Roman Empire

An Enthralling Overview of Imperial Rome

© Copyright 2022 - All rights reserved.

The content contained within this book may not be reproduced, duplicated, or transmitted without direct written permission from the author or the publisher.

Under no circumstances will any blame or legal responsibility be held against the publisher, or author, for any damages, reparation, or monetary loss due to the information contained within this book, either directly or indirectly.

Legal Notice:

This book is copyright protected. It is only for personal use. You cannot amend, distribute, sell, use, quote, or paraphrase any part, or the content within this book, without the consent of the author or publisher.

Disclaimer Notice:

Please note the information contained within this document is for educational and entertainment purposes only. All effort has been executed to present accurate, up-to-date, reliable, and complete information. No warranties of any kind are declared or implied. Readers acknowledge that the author is not engaging in the rendering of legal, financial, medical, or professional advice. The content within this book has been derived from various sources. Please consult a licensed professional before attempting any techniques outlined in this book.

By reading this document, the reader agrees that under no circumstances is the author responsible for any losses, direct or indirect, that are incurred as a result of the use of the information contained within this document, including, but not limited to, errors, omissions, or inaccuracies.

Free limited time bonus

Stop for a moment. We have a free bonus set up for you. The problem is this: we forget 90% of everything that we read after 7 days. Crazy fact, right? Here's the solution: we've created a printable, 1-page pdf summary for this book that you're reading now. All you have to do to get your free pdf summary is to go to the following website: **https://livetolearn.lpages.co/enthrallinghistory/**

Once you do, it will be intuitive. Enjoy, and thank you!

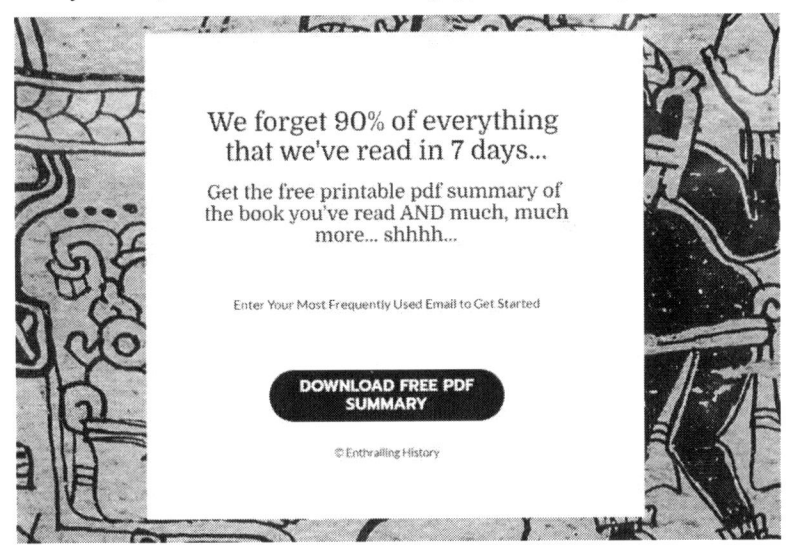

Table of Contents

- INTRODUCTION 1
- CHAPTER 1 – AUGUSTUS AND THE CLAUDIANS 3
- CHAPTER 2 – THE PAX ROMANA 15
- CHAPTER 3 – THE FIVE GOOD EMPERORS 21
- CHAPTER 4 – THE THIRD CENTURY CRISIS........................ 30
- CHAPTER 5 – FROM THE TETRARCHY TO THE FALL OF THE WEST 38
- CHAPTER 6 – TRADE AND TRANSPORTATION 47
- CHAPTER 7 – CENTRAL AND PROVINCIAL GOVERNING ... 57
- CHAPTER 8 – IMPERIAL ARMY AND WARFARE................. 66
- CHAPTER 9 – SOCIAL STRUCTURE AND STATUS............... 76
- CHAPTER 10 – ARTS AND ARCHITECTURE 85
- CHAPTER 11 – DAILY LIFE AND CUSTOMS 96
- CHAPTER 12 – RELIGION AND EDUCATION.................... 107
- CONCLUSION 116
- HERE'S ANOTHER BOOK BY ENTHRALLING HISTORY THAT YOU MIGHT LIKE... 118
- FREE LIMITED TIME BONUS 119
- BIBLIOGRAPHY 120

Introduction

The first civilization sprang to life sometime around 3,500 BCE in Mesopotamia. A couple of centuries later, the Nile began to witness the first signs of settlers on its riverbanks. Later on, the Greeks were born and quickly rose as one of the most influential civilizations to ever exist. Fast forward to over a thousand years later, and the earth saw the emergence of yet another civilization. This time around, it was somewhere around the region of Yangtze, China. It was not until the mid-8th century BCE that the world finally welcomed the Roman civilization, which was believed to have been founded near the Tiber River.

Despite the Romans' late arrival compared, their ancient civilization managed to thrive. Starting with only a small, humble kingdom, the Romans then entered a long yet harsh period of a republic before finally transforming into one of the most powerful empires in the whole world. It encompassed the majority of the European continent, the Mediterranean islands, North Africa, and most parts of West Asia.

Rome, sometimes known as the Eternal City, was the empire's nucleus. In this very city, one could find the emperor's palace. It was also the heart of Rome, as senators would converge there to discuss pressing matters of the state. The Roman Forum, Circus Maximus, and, of course, the well-known Colosseum were all located within the glorious Eternal City. In fact, Rome is widely considered by historians as one of the greatest cities to ever exist in ancient history. Its many surviving structures and records are a constant reminder of how advanced the Roman civilization was back then.

As an empire that never ceased to see the expansion of its frontiers every few years, the Romans were no doubt proud of their military prowess. They experienced more than a dozen defeats throughout the years—Pyrrhus, Hannibal, and Mithridates VI of Pontus were some of ancient Rome's most formidable foes—but the Roman military was known for its strong resilience. Their training would only get harder, as did the punishments, which ensured the soldiers were always ready for another battle. To put it simply, the Romans had absolutely zero knowledge of how to lose, which eventually became the main key to the empire's success.

However, conquest campaigns and battles were not Rome's only pressing matters, as Rome was constantly entangled with its own political issues. The empire was governed by weak and selfish emperors multiple times, which often resulted in chaos. Economic crises, famine, and deadly plagues were also familiar to the Romans; these were some of the factors that nearly crushed the empire to the ground in the 3rd century CE. However, the Roman Empire prevailed and overcame each of the obstacles thrown at them, but the bloody skirmishes and conflicts would never fully end.

This book aims to provide readers with not only an enthralling journey into the events that took place in the Roman Empire but also an interesting overview of how the Romans lived their daily lives within the safe walls of the Eternal City. Discover how Augustus became the Father of Rome, the different social classes and their traditions, the spread of Christianity, and the terrible fall of the Western Roman Empire.

Chapter 1 – Augustus and the Claudians

Julius Caesar is remembered for being one of Rome's greatest generals. It is sometimes hard to remember that he was also human. When a blade stabbed the fifty-five-year-old dictator, he bled. All it took for the dictator to stumble and drop helplessly to the floor was a stab to the neck. After twenty-three stabs gifted by his fellow senators, Julius Caesar finally succumbed to his wounds. His purple toga was drenched in a pool of his blood, and his body was left unattended for a few hours at the base of the Curia of Pompey, as none dared to approach the once glorious dictator for life.

The assassination of Julius Caesar.
https://commons.wikimedia.org/wiki/File:Vincenzo_Camuccini_-_La_morte_di_Cesare.jpg

Words about Caesar's terrible assassination reached nineteen-year-old Gaius Octavius (better known as Octavian), Caesar's grand-nephew, who was undergoing his military studies in Apollonia with his childhood friend, Marcus Vipsanius Agrippa. Some claimed that Octavian was initially hesitant to return to Rome after hearing the news, as he suspected the conspirators might hunt him next, especially since Caesar had no legitimate children by Roman law. However, he later changed his mind after listening to Agrippa's advice.

Octavian set sail to Italy, where he learned the contents of Caesar's will. Aside from leaving two-thirds of his fortune to Octavian, the late dictator had officially adopted Octavian, thus making him his heir. After officially accepting the adoption, Octavian assumed the name Gaius Julius Caesar, which led most of the public to welcome his return warmly. However, one influential figure was not on the same page as the others. His name was Mark Antony. He had been Caesar's closest ally and one of his best generals.

From the very beginning, Octavian never saw eye to eye with Antony. Although Octavian expressed his gratitude to Antony for arranging Caesar's funeral, he also criticized him for pardoning the conspirators. Antony, who consistently underestimated Octavian, fueled the rivalry between them by denying the future emperor's rights to Caesar's fortune—one of the signs that showed Antony's abuse of power.

Some of the senators, especially Marcus Tullius Cicero, Rome's greatest orator and statesman, began to withdraw their support for Antony, as they saw him as yet another power-hungry tyrant. Most of them shifted their focus to Octavian, whom they thought was the lesser evil. Seeing that the growing tension between the two rivals could be put to good use, Cicero composed the *Philippics*, a series of hate speeches condemning Antony in an effort to rally the senators against him. It was successful, as Mark Antony was declared a public enemy soon after.

Octavian, along with two other consuls, Hirtius and Pansa, were dispatched by the Senate to suppress Antony, who was laying siege on Decimus in Cisalpine Gaul. The two consuls, however, lost their lives during the battle, thus giving Octavian an opportunity to showcase his impressive command. Antony's forces were defeated in 43 BCE by Octavian. However, the Senate had no intention of rewarding the future emperor since his growing influence was considered a threat. The command of Rome's legions was granted to Decimus instead of Octavian, while Caesar's main assassins, Cassius and Brutus, were given governorships of Macedonia and Syria.

Seeing that there was no other way to bring Rome back to its glory with the Senate's treacherous decisions, Octavian resorted to an unlikely alliance with Antony and Marcus Aemilius Lepidus, another one of Caesar's close allies and generals. Together, they formed the Second Triumvirate and established the Lex Pedia, a law that punished all of those who were involved in Caesar's assassination. They hunted down every senator who was thought to be involved in the murder and confiscated their fortune—even Cicero, who did not participate in the murder directly, met his fate. The Second Triumvirate soon accomplished their mission when they emerged victorious at the Battle of Philippi, where they put an end to the main conspirators, Cassius and Brutus.

An illustration of the Battle of Actium in 31 BCE.
https://commons.wikimedia.org/wiki/File:The_Battle_of_Actium,_2_September_31BC_R MG_BHC0251.tiff

With Caesar's murderers gone, the Second Triumvirate retained their power over the Roman Republic for years to come. However, Antony's decision to divorce Octavia (Octavian's sister) in favor of the Egyptian queen Cleopatra caused a horrendous stir in Rome. The Senate stripped Antony of his powers and declared war on Cleopatra, which led to the Battle of Actium—the last civil war of the Roman Republic, which eventually resulted in the rise of Octavian as Rome's first emperor.

Learning from his adoptive father's mistake, Octavian was careful not to flaunt his power over Rome, although he was already hailed as a hero after emerging victorious against Antony and Cleopatra. In 27 BCE, Octavian announced his retirement from the political world, to which the Senate disagreed and begged him to take the lead. He was granted the title of Augustus, which translates as the "Revered One." This marks the beginning of the Roman Empire. Although Octavian now held the title of Augustus, he made sure to never address himself with his honorable title, instead using the title of "first citizen."

Under Emperor Augustus's reign, Rome was rewarded with peace, and nearly every aspect of Roman life was changed for the better. Soon, a new taxation system was introduced, along with a census. New laws were passed to ensure both moral and marital stability among the citizens of Rome. According to the ancient Roman historian Cassius Dio, Augustus once banished his only daughter, Julia, to the small island of Pandateria upon discovering her scandalous behavior.

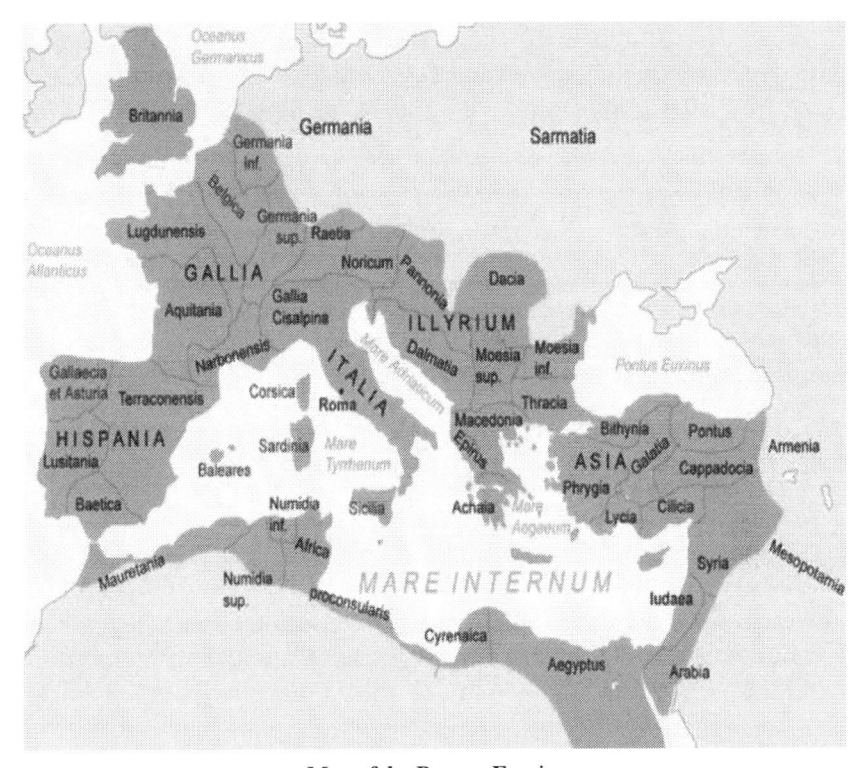

Map of the Roman Empire
Jani Niemenmaa, CC BY-SA 3.0 <http://creativecommons.org/licenses/by-sa/3.0/>, via Wikimedia Commons: https://commons.wikimedia.org/wiki/File:Roman_Empire_Map.png

Augustus's brilliant strategies and commanding skills greatly helped the empire expand its borders. The Roman empire successfully annexed not only Egypt but also a part of Spain and Central Europe, along with regions of the Middle East, including Judaea, which eventually came under direct Roman rule by 6 CE. With more regions and territories in his grasp, the emperor expanded the network of Roman roads and founded Rome's first postal service to ensure better communication over long distances. Police and fire brigades were established during Augustus's reign, as was the Praetorian Guard, an elite force responsible for protecting both the imperial family and Rome.

The empire's economy and arts flourished. Rome saw the birth of the famous Roman Baths; the emperor's closest friend and chief deputy, Marcus Vipsanius Agrippa, designed the empire's first-ever bath. The emperor even renewed various religious practices in Rome and restored a great number of temples, including the

Temple of Jupiter Feretrius, Rome's first-ever temple (now destroyed) was believed to have been built on the Capitoline Hill. In 28 BCE alone, the emperor restored at least eighty-two temples in the city.

Augustus was known for kickstarting the Pax Romana, the golden age of Rome. To honor his great success, the emperor was again bestowed another honorable title in 2 BCE: Pater Patriae or Father of the Country. Augustus faced several assassination plots, although none ever succeeded. He managed to rule the empire until he finally died of natural causes in August 14 CE. The mantle was then passed to his adopted son, Tiberius.

Tiberius Augustus Caesar, the Reluctant Emperor

Tiberius was not Augustus's first option. In fact, the emperor had previously chosen three other heirs to continue his legacy. They were his two grandsons, Lucius and Gaius Caesar, and his nephew, Marcellus. But when the three heirs took turns dying mysteriously—some claimed it was Tiberius's mother, Livia, who pulled the strings and eliminated them from the political arena, though it was never confirmed—Augustus was left with no choice but to shift his focus to his estranged stepson, Tiberius.

Statues of Tiberius and his mother, Livia.
Miguel Hermoso Cuesta, CC BY-SA 4.0 <https://creativecommons.org/licenses/by-sa/4.0>, via Wikimedia Commons: https://commons.wikimedia.org/wiki/File:Livia_y_Tiberio_M.A.N._01.JPG

Tiberius might have been known for his military prowess. After all, he was a successful general who had led the Roman forces to victory in both Armenia and Germany. But as much as he enjoyed commanding his legions, Tiberius had no intention of being in the spotlight of the political world. Nevertheless, he was crowned the empire's second emperor as soon as Augustus gasped his last breath. A year after Tiberius's succession, he became rather absent. Projects were abruptly put on hold, and his relationship with the Senate deteriorated. Few were fond of his rule, something the emperor was aware of.

The paranoia of being overthrown started to cloud Tiberius's judgment. He set his eyes on Germanicus, a brilliant general and the next emperor in line (Tiberius had adopted him per the request of the late Augustus). However, in 18 BCE, Germanicus died suddenly, leaving his wife alone with his six children.

Believing that it was a planned assassination, Germanicus's widow, Agrippina the Elder, accused Tiberius of staging the murder. As a result, Agrippina and her two older sons were killed. Her remaining younger children, Caligula and his sisters, were spared since they posed no real threat to Tiberius. After this incident, Tiberius grew increasingly cruel and would condemn those whom he thought to be against him to death. Treason trials became the norm, and the Romans lived in fear.

In 26 BCE, Tiberius was completely absent from the political arena. He left Rome and moved to Capri, an island off the coast of Italy. While he indulged himself in luxury and scandalous private affairs, the empire's official matters were left entirely to Sejanus, the head of the Praetorian Guard and a ruthless man who sought to take the throne. Eventually, word reached Tiberius, claiming that Sejanus was plotting to eliminate him—after all, Sejanus played a part in the death of Tiberius's favored son, Drusus.

With haste, Tiberius and another Praetorian Guard named Naevius Sutorius Macro (better known as Macro) lured and arrested Sejanus for treason. He was condemned to death right then and there. The ambitious guard was strangled, his limbs torn into pieces and fed to the dogs. The same fate befell his family and loyal followers.

Macro was appointed the new head of the Praetorian Guard, while Caligula was adopted by Tiberius and made his primary heir. But even with the death of Sejanus, the emperor was still not at ease. Treason trials continued to plague the empire, and many Romans died only because of his empty suspicions. Tiberius remained in his villa away from state matters until he died in 37 CE. Some sources claimed his death was orchestrated by Caligula and was killed by Macro, who smothered him to death with a pillow. Tiberius's death was celebrated by many, but peace would not linger in Rome for long.

Caligula, the Mad Emperor

Caligula had no experience in government, diplomacy, or even war when he was named the emperor of Rome. Still, his actions during the first few months of his succession caused the Romans to take a liking to him. To erase the horrors of his predecessor, Caligula stopped the vicious treason trials, recalled the exiles, and freed those whom Tiberius had unjustly captured. Unnecessary tax systems were abolished to the Roman citizens' delight, and long overdue bonuses were awarded to the Praetorian Guard. Most of Tiberius's abandoned projects were revived, with many dilapidated temples successfully restored and new, impressive structures erected all over Rome. To lift the gloomy mood in Rome, Caligula staged a great number of lavish events, such as chariot races, gladiator shows, luxurious banquets, and parties, to entertain his people. At this point, Caligula became the most admired emperor in Rome since the death of Augustus.

However, things took a different turn when the young emperor suffered from a mysterious sickness that almost took his life. Caligula's personality completely changed for the worst; he became almost like his predecessor. Paranoia soon took over the emperor, which led him to reestablish the cruel treason trials. Those whom he suspected to be his enemies were eliminated without question, and he confiscated their fortunes to cover up the deteriorating imperial coffers. Those who were spared from his assassination spree were constantly humiliated and tormented. Even his uncle and co-consul, Claudius, became a laughing stock and relentlessly insulted in front of the Senate. Caligula's extreme madness knew no limits. Not only did he once wage war with the Jewish population in Judea, but he also attempted to appoint Incitatus, his beloved horse, as consul.

The assassination of Caligula.
https://commons.wikimedia.org/wiki/File:The_Assassination_of_the_Emperor_Caligula.jpg

Just like the emperors before him, Caligula had issues with providing a legitimate heir to the throne. Based on certain sources, the mad emperor was desperate for an heir until he resorted to having sexual relations with all three of his sisters; however, this claim remains disputed. Nevertheless, his reign only lasted for four years. In January 41 CE, the Praetorian Guard, spearheaded by Cassius Chaerea, who was one of the many victims of Caligula's ridiculous insults, murdered the emperor in cold blood. To rid Rome of his bloodline, they killed both his wife and his only daughter. Just like that, the empire was free from a bloodthirsty emperor. The next ruler, however, surprised many: it was none other than Caligula's fifty-year-old uncle, Claudius.

Claudius, the Unexpected Emperor

Claudius's ascension to the throne was unlike any of his predecessors. Instead of having his name written in the will of the previous emperor, Claudius was proclaimed emperor by the Praetorian Guard, who stumbled upon him cowering and quivering behind a set of curtains after witnessing Caligula's death. In his early life, Claudius was described by his own blood relatives, including his mother, as a fool. Despite being the grandson of Augustus, Claudius was thought by many to be dimwitted. That was, however, until he admitted that it was all an act for him to remain alive while Caligula was on the throne.

The Praetorian Guard proclaiming the terrified Claudius as the next emperor.
https://commons.wikimedia.org/wiki/File:Proclaiming_claudius_emperor.png

Claudius was an unpopular candidate in the eyes of the Senate, so his efficiency was doubted. However, he began to shine when he took action against Caligula's murderers. Cassius Chaerea and a few of the conspirators were executed. Not wasting any time, the emperor moved to restore the peace in Rome. He reestablished the law, abolished the treason trials, built a handful of new structures, including a harbor in Ostia, and held gladiatorial games to entertain the people. When a riot broke out due to the extreme food shortage after a long drought, Claudius took the initiative to import grains and feed his subjects.

The empire also went through a major expansion. Several provinces were put under direct Roman rule. His biggest triumph was the conquest of Britannia, which had long been a target of Rome due to its wealth. To prove himself as a highly capable ruler, Claudius left Rome and led his army into Britain.

But, of course, like the emperors before him, Claudius had a dark side. When he was forced to face a revolt led by the governor of Upper Illyricum, the emperor grew paranoid. Although the revolt was easily stopped—with many of the participants executed—Claudius grew uneasy with those around him. Those whom he suspected of holding ill intentions toward him were killed or forced to commit suicide.

Other than his unfortunate luck in political matters during the last few years of his reign, the emperor was also unlucky with his marriages. Claudius was said to have married four times, but it was his marriage to Agrippina the Younger that cost him his life. Agrippina, who was also his niece, was hell-bent on seeing her son, Nero, ascend the imperial throne. While some suggest that Claudius died of old age in 54 CE, others believe his wife poisoned him. With Claudius no longer in the picture, the mantle was passed to Nero, just as his mother had dreamed.

Nero, the Emperor Who Entertains

Nero, the last of the Julio-Claudian emperors, was put on the throne at the age of sixteen and ruled over the vast empire for fourteen miserable years. During his first years as emperor, his people often described him as a generous and kind-hearted man who genuinely cared for his subjects. In an effort to remove the footsteps left by his adoptive father, Nero abolished a majority of Claudius's edicts and reduced the taxes. Games, concerts, plays, and chariot races were frequently held, as the emperor was fond of entertainment. He restored the power and importance of the Senate, not only to strengthen his power but also so he could diverge from his responsibilities and pursue his private interests: singing and playing the lyre. It was said that whenever the emperor was performing, none of the audience was permitted to leave, no matter how bad it was.

As time passed, the emperor began to participate in things other than musical performances. When he grew restless with his mother, who claimed to be the true force behind the throne, Nero was quick to plan her murder. Two murder attempts were made, but Agrippina survived each time. However, the third attempt was a success; Agrippina was killed by her own son. His mother was not the only victim; Nero also got his hands dirty by killing his wives and unborn child.

Later on, another set of events caused Nero's life to go into turmoil. An unsuccessful coup, combined with a failed revolt in Britain, led the emperor into paranoia—just like the emperors before him. The biggest cause of Nero's downfall was the Great Fire of Rome, which engulfed 70 percent of the city. While hundreds of people succumbed to the fire, were left homeless, and were sent into chaos, the emperor was said to have watched from the safety of his palace while playing his lyre. The blame was put on the shoulders of the Christians.

The Great Fire of Rome, 64 CE.
https://commons.wikimedia.org/wiki/File:Robert,_Hubert_-_Incendie_%C3%A0_Rome_-.jpg

Although Rome was rebuilt soon after, Nero had seriously drained the treasury. Seeing the disasters that fell upon the city under his watch, the Senate declared him a public enemy, which led to his suicide at the ripe age of thirty. With Nero gone, the Romans trampled out of their homes, celebrating. Nero's death marked the end of the Julio-Claudian dynasty.

Chapter 2 – The Pax Romana

Many are familiar with or at least have heard of the main ancient Roman gods and goddesses, which included Jupiter, Neptune, Minerva, and Mars. Janus, on the other hand, is a rather mysterious Roman deity due to the lack of surviving information. Historians have tried to discover the god's origins, but unfortunately, only more mysteries and questions surfaced. Janus's depiction on Rome's oldest coin clearly indicates that he was one of the oldest gods in the Roman pantheon. The first month of the year, January, is said to have been derived from the ancient god's name. Janus was invoked at the start of every religious ceremony, and the first portion of a sacrifice had to be dedicated to him before the others. Yet, only a few shrines and statues were ever erected to honor him.

A part of a sculpture of the two-headed god Janus.
Loudon dodd, CC BY-SA 3.0 <https://creativecommons.org/licenses/by-sa/3.0>, via Wikimedia Commons: https://commons.wikimedia.org/wiki/File:Janus1.JPG

The only well-known building dedicated to the obscure deity was the Temple of Janus. Commissioned by Rome's second king, Numa Pompilius, the temple, more accurately classified as a shrine, stood at the center of the Eternal City. The shrine was built to house only a bronze statue of the two-headed Janus. Its most prominent feature was the double doors, which the Romans often referred to as the Gates of War. The gates were left open when Rome was plagued with continuous warfare and would only be closed if peace was achieved—a rare occasion, according to the philosopher and biographer Plutarch, as the Eternal City was almost always in the midst of violent battles and bloodshed due to its constant expansion.

While the reason behind the closing and opening of the gates vary (some sources believe that leaving the gates open during active conflicts allowed the deity to watch over them), historians and experts are sure the gates were only closed twice since the foundation of Rome. Numa first closed it upon reaching peace during his reign, followed by the Roman commander Aulus Manlius Torquatus Atticus after gaining victory during the First Punic War. The gates were opened when the Gauls invaded northern Italy, and they would remain open for four hundred years until Augustus came along.

Before the arrival of Augustus, the Roman Republic had never experienced long-term peace. War raged without rest, worrying its people day and night. Later on, a series of never-ending civil wars broke out among influential figures who craved ultimate power. Marius, Sulla, Caesar, Crassus, Pompey, and Mark Antony were some of the most notable Roman figures who wished to seize power over the already chaotic republic. By this point in history, it is safe to assume that peace was far from the Romans' reach. However, the arrival of the late dictator's adopted son changed things. A sigh of relief could be had for the first time in four centuries, as peace was finally possible.

Despite his young age, Augustus had his heart set on continuing Julius Caesar's legacy. Witnessing all of the threats and catastrophes that befell the republic, the future emperor was left with no choice but to introduce new political reforms. This was not a simple task; achieving peace and restoring Rome to its glory would no doubt be time-consuming. The young emperor was also well aware that he had gained a great number of enemies, but he was ready to face anyone who dared to step in his way, including Mark Antony.

Despite having to battle a mysterious illness that sometimes forced him to remain in bed and away from ongoing wars, Augustus managed to showcase his exceptional skills and abilities to lead, thus earning him the support of many. When Mark Antony and his beloved Egyptian queen went a step too far, Augustus led his army against them without hesitation. The battle went down in history as one of the most important events in the ancient world, as it not only took the life of both Mark Antony and Cleopatra but also marked the end of the Roman Republic and the beginning of a new era.

Upon returning to the Eternal City, Augustus ordered the closing of the Gates of Janus in 29 BCE to signify peace. The long series of unrest and civil wars were finally brought to an end with the death of Mark Antony, one of Rome's greatest generals. The crowds cheered as Rome was ushered into its golden era, known as the Pax Romana (the "Roman Peace").

For the first time in history, ancient Rome enjoyed a period of relative peace for more than a few decades. The Pax Romana was believed to have lasted for nearly two centuries, starting from the reign of the first emperor, Augustus, until the death of Marcus Aurelius, the last of the Five Good Emperors, in 180 CE. During this time, Rome was at its peak. The empire underwent a massive territorial expansion alongside the rapid growth of its population; under the reign of Augustus alone, the empire consisted of about sixty million people.

However, not everyone was happy with the sudden peace. During the early years of the Pax Romana, many Romans were said to have struggled to adapt. Ever since the early foundation of Rome back in the 8th century BCE, the city was always intertwined with warfare to the point where its people began to see it as a form of might and power. The absence of constant battles and conquests somehow worried the Romans. To them, warfare was a good thing; they gained wealth by winning wars, and their reputation grew every time their enemies lay dead on the battlefield. This was one of the many issues that Augustus had to deal with the moment he accepted the responsibility of leading the people. In an effort to persuade his people to accept the Pax Romana with open arms, the young emperor came up with a series of propaganda campaigns. He assured the Romans that peace was the best way to achieve prosperity.

The Pax Romana was a relative peace; the empire was not entirely free from wars and battles. To put it in simple words, the Pax Romana was an era where the Romans had to face little to no internal skirmishes. Its people, especially those in power, were no longer at each other's throats, and large-scale civil wars were a thing of the past. Fewer soldiers were stationed at the heart of the empire, with most of the legions being sent to places that were likely to be in danger, such as the imperial frontier.

Wars and foreign forces at the empire's borders continued to exist during the Roman Peace. The Pax Romana did not mean the Romans completely sheathed their weapons. Military missions and campaigns were still launched; Augustus even went on several conquests to capture new regions in an effort to further expand the empire. Under his reign, captured provinces were allowed to exercise their local customs, traditions, and religious practices as long as they did not violate Roman law and as long as they chose to comply with Roman taxation and military control. Augustus even kept his eyes open for corrupt provincial governors; those who were caught exploiting their power for their own benefit were quickly punished.

Just as Augustus had promised his people, the empire's economy and trade skyrocketed during this era of peace. Long-distance trade flourished, especially when the Mediterranean was free of threats. The emperor ordered the Roman navy to launch an attack against pirates, making the sea safer for traders to enter and exit the harbors. Since Roman traders and merchants could sail farther east without having to fear for their safety, they were able to bring back precious gems and exquisite silks. Apart from jewelry, the Romans, typically the nobles and the rich, were very fond of silk; Emperor Heliogabalus, who ruled in 218 CE, was believed to have refused to wear clothing unless they were made out of silk. Export activities also boomed during this period of history, as the Romans could find more markets for their goods, which included wines, textiles, pottery, glass, and other construction materials.

With economic stability, the imperial government was able to invest in many major construction projects. The Romans are well known for their road networks, and Augustus commissioned the expansion of road systems throughout the empire, which no doubt benefited the movement of the legions. Information and mail could also arrive in a shorter amount of time. By the end of Emperor Augustus's reign, over eighty kilometers (fifty miles) of new roads had been constructed. Bridges, harbors, and aqueducts were also often built by the emperors who ruled during the golden age.

Apart from architecture and the economy, the Pax Romana witnessed the birth of many Roman poets and writers. Horace, Virgil, Tibullus, and Ovid are some of the most memorable Roman writers that thrived during this era. Despite being renowned for his exceptional works of poetry, the latter was sentenced to exile by Augustus due to the production of erotic poetry and opinions of the emperor's private life and marriage. However, the poet did not stop writing even after his exile; he wrote two more collections of poetry that told the stories of his sadness and desolation. Exiled for life, Ovid died in 17 CE, but his influence on poetry has lived on; Shakespeare was among the many modern authors to have been influenced by the exiled poet.

Ovid banished from Rome.
https://commons.wikimedia.org/wiki/File:Turner_Ovid_Banished_from_Rome.jpg

"I found Rome of bricks; I leave to you one of marble."

These were the words of Augustus Caesar during the last years of his life. Rome had indeed been near shambles when it passed into his hands, but the emperor successfully brought it back to its glory. One might even say he turned it into one of the most prosperous empires of all time. From a broken republic filled with nothing but a series of civil wars, Rome transformed itself into an empire that stretched as far as Britannia and Egypt. The death of Rome's first emperor caused a stir, as several problems arose during the reigns of the next few emperors. However, the Pax Romana was not broken, and the Eternal City continued to experience relative peace.

During Nero's reign, the people of Rome began to sense another catastrophe heading toward them. After the end of the Julio-Claudian dynasty, the city faced a few pressing matters that put a crack in the Roman Peace, but the era of the Five Good Emperors successfully reversed the damages and made the empire prosper again. The peace in the Eternal City was extended for a few more decades before it finally cracked and crumbled to pieces in 180 CE.

Chapter 3 – The Five Good Emperors

The last emperor of the Julio-Claudian dynasty, Nero, contributed to the many pressing issues that had taken over the Roman Empire. His death was celebrated by not only the Senate but also the suffering commoners of different social classes. With the throne now empty, the empire was put under the care of an emperor who founded a whole new dynasty. It was known as the Flavian dynasty, and it consisted of only three emperors: Vespasian, Titus, and Domitian.

The most popular among those three was Domitian. Early in his reign, the emperor portrayed great potential to lead the empire out of its troubles. He did not ignore the welfare of his people and rebuilt the city, which had been destroyed after the Great Fire. Unlike his brother, Titus, Domitian was not known for his military skills, but he spearheaded a few successful campaigns during his reign. Unfortunately, just like many of Rome's great emperors, Domitian succumbed to extreme paranoia. In 96 CE, the emperor was brutally killed at the hands of a group of conspirators. Instead of mourning the loss of their emperor, the Senate was overjoyed. Once again, Rome was free from the grasp of yet another insanely paranoid leader. Without wasting time, they announced a new emperor to the throne. His name was Nerva, and he was the first of Rome's Five Good Emperors.

Nerva (r. 96–98 CE)

The new emperor was rather old when he was put in charge of the vast empire; he was almost sixty-six. No one would have expected Nerva to take the mantle; he was not very popular among the Romans. Although he had spent the majority of his life serving the empire during the reigns of both the Julio-Claudian and Flavian dynasties, achieving great success, Nerva never gained any prominence. The Senate did not even plan to bestow him the power permanently; he was only hailed as emperor to fill the vacancy until the Senate could decide on someone with greater influence and potential.

After years of serving the empire behind the scenes, Nerva began to shine and eventually earned a spot among the public after voicing his promise to return liberty to the Romans. He ended the treason trials that had left the Romans cowering in fear, returned the properties confiscated by Domitian back to the senators, showered the common people with generous gifts, and lowered the taxes. He earned the support of many, but his generosity also depleted the imperial coffers to the point where the empire was almost on the verge of bankruptcy.

Another challenge that Nerva had to face was the military's rage, as the soldiers and officers preferred his predecessor. Upon learning that Nerva had no plans to prosecute the conspirators who took Domitian's life, the Praetorian Guard launched a siege on the imperial palace and demanded the assassins be held accountable. Instead of complying with the violent request, Nerva offered his own neck to slit—an action completely ignored by the Praetorian Guard, who chose to spare the emperor and slaughter the conspirators.

After the siege, Nerva was left shaken to his core—he even thought of stepping down from the throne at one point. He was well aware that his authority was beginning to decline, especially without the support of the military. Knowing that he could lose his life to anyone around him, the emperor began to think of a possible heir to succeed him.

Since he had no child of his own—some say he never even married—Nerva adopted the governor of Upper Germany, Marcus Ulpius Traianus, as his son. In January 98 CE, a day after Nerva died of natural causes, his adopted son rose as the next emperor of the Nerva-Antonine dynasty.

Trajan (r. 98–117 CE)

Marcus Ulpius Traianus was the second emperor of Rome not to be born in Italy; he was born in Hispania. After receiving news that his adoptive father had passed away and that the mantle would be passed to him, Traianus did not return to Rome straightaway. Instead, he stayed with his legions in Germany in case the barbarians invaded. It was only in early 99 CE that he journeyed back to Rome and participated in an official ceremony that declared him the next emperor.

A bust of Trajan.
https://commons.wikimedia.org/wiki/File:Traianus_Glyptothek_Munich_72.jpg

Now known by the name Trajan, the emperor received a warm welcome from nearly everyone in Rome, especially the military, given his strong influence on the battlefield. Some might even claim that Trajan was one of the few emperors who mimicked the rule of the great Augustus Caesar. Generous gifts were distributed to the people regardless of their status, and he sponsored multiple public games to keep the citizens entertained. However, he did not spend too much on the military. In fact, he only gave them half of what previous emperors before him had given. Since Trajan was already favored in the army due to his long service as a military officer before stepping on the throne, he did not receive backlash from his decision to tone down their payments. Trajan maintained a great relationship with the Senate by bestowing a certain amount of authority over the empire upon them, although his power was still considered supreme.

Even before he took the reins, Trajan had wished to expand the empire. So, when he finally had the opportunity to rule, the emperor decided to fulfill his ambition by launching two wars against Dacia (modern-day Romania and Moldova). Peace between Dacia and Rome was first bought about by Domitian, who had agreed to pay tribute to the king of Dacia, Decebalus. Trajan, however, was completely against this treaty. In the aftermath of the two wars, the capital of Dacia was destroyed. Despite his efforts to defend his kingdom, Decebalus committed suicide. With the victory, the empire expanded. Dacia was made into a Roman province, providing the Romans with valuable supplies of gold and metal, which they used to mint coins.

Trajan also oversaw the construction of a long bridge across the Danube River and into Dacia, which ensured easier access for his army. The solid stone bridge was not the only massive construction project launched during his reign. After acquiring resources from Dacia, the emperor commissioned the construction of various structures, roads, and highways in Rome and its surrounding cities. The *alimenta*, a welfare program founded by Nerva to assist orphans and poor children in the empire, was also carried on by Trajan.

In 113, Trajan yet again showed his mighty potential by strategizing the conquest of Parthia. After assembling the strongest soldiers, Trajan deployed them to invade Parthia, which was in the midst of a civil war. He managed to get his hands on Mesopotamia in 117, but his objective to conquer Parthia failed. In the same year, the sixty-three-year-old emperor fell terribly sick while defending the empire's borders and died.

Hadrian (r. 117–138 CE)

The third emperor of the Nerva-Antonine dynasty was Publius Aelius Hadrianus. Better known as Hadrian, he was a remarkable military officer who began to rise through the ranks in 91 CE. He served as tribune during the reign of Emperor Nerva and was handpicked to travel to Gaul by the end of 97 CE to relay the news of Trajan's adoption and his possible ascension to the throne.

Hadrian's rise to the throne, like his predecessor, was welcomed by the Romans. He was seen as a charismatic, honest, and peaceful leader by the public.

Despite Hadrian's long tenure in the military, he was not keen on conquests; instead, he wanted to consolidate the empire's defenses. He put a stop to Trajan's campaign in Parthia and planned peace negotiations. To achieve peace, the Romans withdrew from Armenia, leaving it a neutral state. Although this decision was not liked by many, especially those who had loyally served under Trajan, it saved the empire from further damage and made it even stronger than before.

Image: The remains of Hadrian's Wall.
https://commons.wikimedia.org/wiki/File:Milecastle_39_on_Hadrian%27s_Wall.jpg

Hadrian believed that the empire had reached its maximum extent and that the most crucial thing to focus on was its border security. He wished for the empire's stability and prosperity. So, instead of staying in Rome and planning strategy after strategy for a new conquest, Hadrian chose to leave the imperial palace and travel throughout the provinces to oversee the provincial administration. The emperor was said to have visited every single province in the empire by the year 133 and recognized where he needed to eliminate corruption. He also commissioned multiple construction projects. His greatest contribution was the great Hadrian's Wall in Britain, which was built for defensive purposes. The borders near Germany were also strengthened under his rule.

Hadrian was also a man of culture. During his travels across the provinces, he promoted the importance of culture to his people. Some sources claim that the emperor was fond of Greece and that he visited the province more than once during his reign. Unlike the other Roman emperors who preferred clean-shaven faces, Hadrian sported a Greek-style beard. Hadrian sponsored many poetry contests in Rome and was known for founding the city of Antinoöpolis on the banks of the Nile to honor his deceased lover, Antinous. Although Hadrian claimed that Antinous's death was accidental—he had drowned in the Nile—other scholars, including Cassius Dio, believed the young boy had performed a sacrificial ceremony to cure Hadrian's mysterious illness.

Hadrian's grief did not stop him from running the empire. He grew short-tempered as time passed, but he soon projected his anger on the Jews who had started a revolt in Judea. His solution to the revolt was to annihilate the Jews in the region. A thousand towns and villages were burned in the process, and nearly sixty thousand Jews were slaughtered, while others were banished. Afterward, Hadrian renamed Judea Syria Palaestina and turned it into a Roman city, further suppressing Jewish beliefs.

During his last few years, Hadrian remained in his luxurious villa away from Rome. He spent most of his time writing poetry while overseeing the empire's administration. His health declined, and in 138, Hadrian died due to a heart attack.

Antoninus Pius (r. 138–161 CE)

Having no child of his own, Hadrian resorted to adoption. He initially had his eyes on the consul Lucius Ceionius Commodus, but things quickly went south as soon as Lucius was appointed governor and sent to Pannonia. He suffered from tuberculosis and died in January 138. Thus, Hadrian was forced to search for another heir. This time around, he had his eyes on Marcus Aurelius. He somehow could see Aurelius's capabilities, but unfortunately, he was only sixteen at the time, which was too young to hold such power over the empire. Running out of time, Hadrian, who was already on his deathbed, finally announced Antoninus Pius, his most trusted advisor, as his successor.

Many thought Antoninus would rule for only a short amount of time, at least until Aurelius could reach an age fit to rule, especially after he agreed to adopt both Marcus Aurelius and Lucius Verus as his successors. Plus, he was already reaching the age of fifty, so most thought that it would not be too long before he passed the throne to his adoptive sons. Much to everyone's surprise, the emperor lived a long life. Although Antoninus was not as popular as his predecessor, the Romans began to show their support when they saw his unexpected efficiency and drive.

Emperor Antoninus in his military garb.
Jean-Pol GRANDMONT, CC BY-SA 3.0 <https://creativecommons.org/licenses/by-sa/3.0>, *via Wikimedia Commons:* https://commons.wikimedia.org/wiki/File:0_Antoninus_Pius_-_Museo_Chiaramonti_(Vatican).JPG

The new emperor took the reins when the empire was at its peak. The economy was blossoming. No political unrest or civil wars could be seen. The borders were well secured, and famine was a thing of the past. Liberty had been achieved, with the people of all classes living without fear. To ensure his position was never challenged, Antoninus maintained his relationship with almost everyone, be it the Senate, the military, nobles, and even the commoners. He even passed legislation that protected the rights of slaves and increased the chances of them obtaining their freedom.

Continuing Hadrian's legacy, Antoninus focused on upgrading Rome's infrastructure. He issued orders to complete Hadrian's many construction projects, although he had his own projects as well. The Temple of the Deified Hadrian and the Temple of the Deified Faustina were some of the impressive structures commissioned by Antoninus. The Colosseum was also restored during his rule. Following Hadrian's footsteps, the emperor issued the construction of the Antonine Wall, which took nearly twelve years to complete.

Antoninus was described as an even-tempered emperor. The empire was indeed at peace, as little to zero wars and conflicts took place during Antoninus's reign. After ruling for over twenty years, the emperor finally passed away at the age of seventy-four due to a fever. His remains were laid in Hadrian's Mausoleum, right next to his beloved wife and sons.

Marcus Aurelius (r. 161–180 CE)

Antoninus Pius was said to have properly groomed Marcus Aurelius to prepare him as his successor. So, when Marcus Aurelius's adoptive father passed away in 161, he was hailed as the new emperor, just as Hadrian intended a few decades prior. However, Aurelius, now at the age of forty, had to share his power with Lucius Verus, whom the Senate had announced as his co-emperor; this was the first time Rome had ever recognized two ruling emperors at the same time. But since Marcus was older than his adoptive brother, he held more power.

By the time they both rose to power, trouble had begun to brew across the empire. The Parthians decided to invade Armenia as soon as they learned of Antoninus's death. At the same time, the empire was faced with possible threats by people living in what is today Britain and Germany after decades of peace. Ever since he was young, Marcus had been groomed to be an efficient leader; however, he was never given any military experience. He was more fond of philosophy—his writings called *Meditations* can still be read today.

Nevertheless, he devoted himself to military studies to prepare for the upcoming threats. Lucius was supposed to soothe the ongoing war with the Parthians but instead stayed behind the city walls, which ultimately led the campaign into a stalemate. Thanks to his subordinate, Avidius Cassius, Rome eventually emerged victorious.

In 166, Marcus had to put everything he learned from his military studies on the battlefield when he was faced with multiple Germanic tribes that managed to pierce through the Roman frontiers and destroy several villages. Although their raids were devastating, the Roman army successfully put a stop to their advance. Warfare and invasions were not the worst events to happen during Marcus's reign, as the Antonine Plague terrorized the empire. Millions were killed in this catastrophe, including Lucius Verus.

Now the sole emperor of Rome, Marcus Aurelius put all of his efforts into seeing the empire flourish again. Some even claimed the emperor always placed the needs of his people before anything else. Despite not liking military life, he continued to defend the empire against threats. He nearly ended the continuous war with the Germanic tribes, but in 180, Marcus Aurelius perished in his military quarters due to unknown reasons.

His death marked the end of the era of the Five Good Emperors. Although great stability and peace had been restored by the five emperors of the Nerva-Antonine dynasty, Rome was forced to face many wars and political unrest in the decades to come.

Chapter 4 – The Third Century Crisis

The Romans knew the days of the Five Good Emperors were gone when they received the news of the devastating death of fifty-eight-year-old Marcus Aurelius. The Eternal City was entrusted in the hands of Commodus, who had already served the empire as joint emperor alongside Aurelius. Despite being the only son of the great Marcus Aurelius, Commodus was not a favorite among his subjects. He had endured many assassination attempts, and when his associate succumbed to one of the murderous plots, Commodus became paranoid. Many perished due to his suspicions—he even had a list of those he'd execute next—but in 192, Commodus was successfully murdered, strangled by a wrestler hired by the conspirators.

Commodus strangled by the Roman wrestler Narcissus.
https://commons.wikimedia.org/wiki/File:Commodus_is_strangled_by_Narcissus.png

    The death of Commodus did not solve the political unrest in the empire. In 193, Rome was yet again plunged into a period of civil war when five rulers fought for a chance to be crowned the next Caesar. The paranoid Commodus was succeeded by Pertinax, who portrayed far better qualities compared to his predecessor. However, his disagreements with the Praetorian Guard led to his death eighty-six days after his ascension. Afterward, three more men took turns claiming the throne before Septimius Severus finally took the mantle and ended the Year of the Five Emperors. With Severus as emperor, another dynasty was born: the Severan dynasty, which would rule the empire for over forty-two years and saw the beginning of the Third Century Crisis.

    Taking a lesson from Pertinax, who the Praetorian Guard assassinated after refusing to come to terms with them, Severus quenched the military's possible disobedience by awarding them increased pay. Each soldier was paid at least five hundred denarii—a major increase from their previous salary of three hundred denarii annually. This decision was not a problem until the empire was enlarged even more; Severus successfully launched a campaign in Africa and Britain. More armed forces were required to defend the borders from foreign invasions, which meant more payments must be made to secure their service. To curb the issue, Severus debased the currency by decreasing the percentage of silver in the coinage, a method that was practiced by future emperors and extended the economic crisis.

While fulfilling the military demands played a part in keeping Severus in power, his dependence on the soldiers' loyalty proved to be a dangerous game. The military's role increased tenfold and shook not only the Senate but also the supreme standing of the emperor.

In 231, the Sassanid Empire, led by Ardashir I, invaded the Roman provinces of the east after successfully bringing down already-weakened Parthia a few years back. This threat left Severus Alexander, the last emperor of the Severan dynasty, with no other choice but to plan a retaliation. There are a few contradicting accounts that tell the story of the battle, but many suggest that despite experiencing heavy casualties and terrible setbacks, the Roman Empire's borders were secured and Ardashir's conquest was stopped. However, Severus Alexander was beginning to lose the support of his troops, especially during the invasion of Germanic tribes in 235.

Some claimed that Severus Alexander was only a puppet while his mother, Julia Mamaea, was the real power. Instead of fighting off the invaders on the battlefield, Severus Alexander made a fatal mistake by following his mother's advice. Julia had advised him to buy the peace, an action considered unacceptable and highly dishonorable to his legions. Severus Alexander and his mother were assassinated by his commanders, marking the beginning of the Third Century Crisis, a fifty-year period where the Roman Empire almost collapsed.

The economic crisis remained one of the empire's biggest concerns, and the military became the real source of power after the murder of Severus Alexander. The Roman Empire saw the succession of more than twenty-five barrack emperors over the span of almost five decades. Instead of rising to the throne through traditional adoptions by previous emperors or having their names written in wills, these barrack emperors were chosen based on their popularity within a military troop. Maximinus Thrax, who was the commander of a legion raised by Severus Alexander, was chosen as the next emperor, though he would be killed by his own troops three years later after failing to prove himself as an effective leader amidst the constant warfare, economic unrest, and famine.

The empire was also in the middle of battling a number of invasions by foreign enemies. The provinces along the Rhine-Danube frontiers were facing heavy threats imposed by the Germanic tribes: the Goths, Vandals, and Alemanni. Seeing that the empire was overwhelmed by the Germanic tribes, the Sassanid Empire—now led by Shapur I, the son of Ardashir—set its eyes on exploiting the Roman Empire's weakness and asserting control over the Levant in the east. In 252, Shapur I gained power over Nisibis and successfully seized Antioch the next year after defeating the Roman army.

With the eastern border in shambles, the barrack emperor Valerian left his son and co-emperor, Gallienus, in control of the west while he marched against the ruthless Sassanid Empire. Personally leading his troops, Valerian arrived in Asia Minor in 259 but was thrown into another battle when he came face to face with the Gothic tribes that were busy invading the region. Little is known about the battle, but historians suggest that the emperor managed to continue his march against Shapur I. Valerian's seventy thousand men soon clashed swords with Shapur's forty thousand men in Edessa. The Roman emperor was utterly defeated and made prisoner; Valerian was the first-ever Roman emperor to get captured and imprisoned by an enemy. He perished the following year.

Foreign attacks were not the only pressing matter terrorizing the empire. When Gallienus rose as the next emperor following his father's death, a rebellion erupted, although he managed to extinguish it in 260. Another obstacle arose when the Germanic tribes invaded northern Italy. With only 60,000 troops at his command, the emperor successfully defeated the 300,000 barbarians; it was said the victory was achieved thanks to his exceptional cavalry troops. Despite the triumph, the emperor was forced to face yet another rebellion. At the same time, Postumus, a well-respected administrator who had defended Germania from several invasions, declared his independence. Modeled after the central government of the Roman Empire, he formed the Gallic Empire, which was made up of Gaul, Britannia, and eventually Hispania.

The eastern provinces of the Roman Empire were secured by Septimius Odaenathus, an aristocrat from the Roman colony Palmyra. He laid an attack on Shapur's army in 260 and emerged victorious. The foreign forces were pushed back to their capital, and by 263, the lands that had once been lost to the Sassanid Empire were safely returned to the Romans. Gallienus appreciated Odaenathus's remarkable success in securing the eastern borders and awarded him with the title of *corrector totius Orientis* or governor of all the east. Odaenathus preferred another title: King of Kings. While remaining a loyal Roman vassal, Odaenathus continued to drive away the foreign invaders who dared to set foot in the eastern provinces. That was, however, until late 267 CE when he and his son were mysteriously assassinated. His widow soon took control and became regent to their underage son.

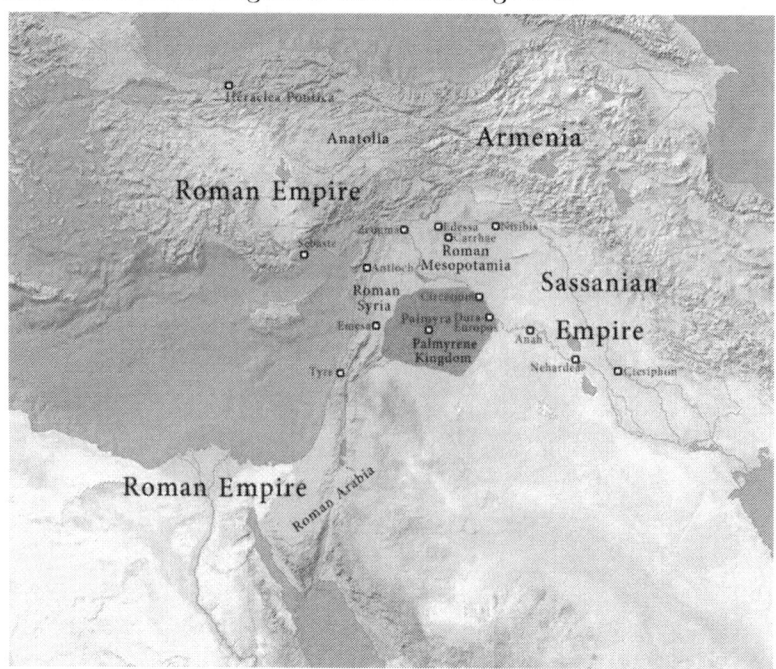

Regions under the authority of Odaenathus of Palmyra.
Attar-Aram syria, CC BY-SA 4.0 <https://creativecommons.org/licenses/by-sa/4.0>, via Wikimedia Commons: https://commons.wikimedia.org/wiki/File:Odaenathus_Kingdom.png

In 265, Gallienus turned his attention to Postumus and his newly formed Gallic Empire. Although sources claimed that Postumus never intended to invade the Roman Empire, Gallienus was ready to face him and reclaim the provinces. The battle was at its peak when Gallienus laid siege on an unnamed city in the Gallic Empire. However, luck was running out for the emperor, as he was pierced by an arrow, forcing him to leave the ongoing battle. The Gallic Empire remained independent. Gallienus managed to heal from his severe wound, only to be assassinated three years later.

The throne then belonged to Claudius II, who also had his eyes on the Gallic Empire. As he prepared to march on Postumus's empire, the emperor was forced to change his plans after receiving news about an invasion of modern-day Serbia by the Goths. With haste, the Romans engaged in a battle with the invaders near Naissus in 269. Even with the exceptional cavalry units led by the future emperor Aurelian, the fierce battle inflicted extreme casualties on both sides. The Romans eventually won the battle after successfully tricking the Goths into a brutal ambush. In the aftermath of the devastating battle, the Goths were said to have lost at least fifty thousand lives. Claudius II became known as the "Conqueror of the Goths."

The same year, Rome was threatened by yet another invasion attempt, this time by the Alemanni at Lake Benacus. Just as in the previous battle, the Romans managed to overpower them and drive them out of the empire. Sometime later, Claudius II received news that likely eased his mind. The founder of the Gallic Empire, Postumus, had been killed. Sensing an opportunity to seize the Gallic provinces, Claudius quickly moved his troops to Hispania. The emperor showed great promise as a leader, but after his success in recapturing Hispania, he lost his life to the Plague of Cyprian.

While the late Claudius II had his hands full putting his life on the line to reclaim the Gallic provinces and defend the Roman Empire from further invasions, Zenobia, regent and queen of Palmyra in the east, was trying to cement her authority. When the news of Claudius's sudden death reached her, she took the opportunity to proclaim her son, Vaballathus, as emperor. Through Zenobia's efforts, the Palmyrene Empire was born. By 271, Egypt and most regions of central and eastern Anatolia were absorbed into the empire. The reason behind this independence is uncertain; some claim that Zenobia was becoming less confident with Roman protection, while others suggest that she simply intended to strengthen the dominance of Palmyrene.

Back in the west, the imperial throne was passed to Aurelian, a battle-hardened soldier who was soon known as the emperor who reunited the Roman Empire. The new emperor took the reins when Rome was shrouded in multiple threats from foreign tribes and independent empires. He was well aware that he had to secure the loyalty of the military before he could march to the battlefield and exterminate the vicious barbarians. By seizing control of the imperial mint in modern-day Croatia, Aurelian managed to gain enough gold coins to distribute to his army. With their loyalty firmly in his hands, Aurelian could begin his battles.

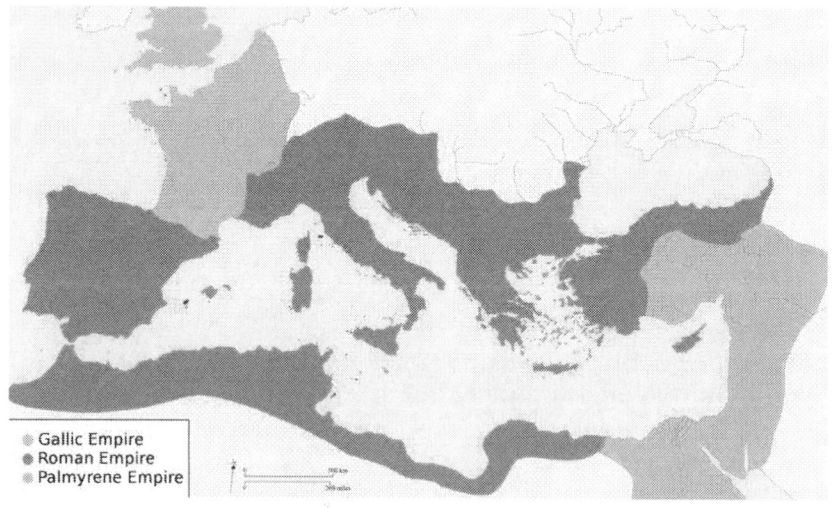

The Roman Empire before Aurelian's reconquest campaigns of the Palmyrene and Gallic Empires.
Blank map of South Europe and North Africa.svg: historicair 23:27, 8 August 2007 (UTC), CC BY-SA 2.5 <https://creativecommons.org/licenses/by-sa/2.5>, via Wikimedia Commons: https://commons.wikimedia.org/wiki/File:Map_of_Ancient_Rome_271_AD.svg

Not wasting a single opportunity, the emperor destroyed the Vandals who had been invading northern Italy. He also led his legions to face the Juthungi, who were already planning to leave Italy with their precious plunder. However, Aurelian managed to intercept the tribe, which led to a battle on the Metaurus River. Aurelian and his troops were victorious; however, another concerning matter surfaced that required his immediate attention.

Rome was thrown into a grain crisis when the Palmyrene Empire successfully claimed Egypt. Aiming to put a stop to Zenobia's growing influence, Aurelian journeyed to the east in 272. The emperor faced little resistance, as most cities of the Palmyrene Empire decided to open their gates to him when he offered mercy. This peaceful strategy did not last long, as he was left with no choice but to engage in a military battle with Zenobia's forces. In less than a year, the emperor emerged victorious. Zenobia and her son attempted to escape but were captured and paraded through the streets of Rome in a triumph held by Aurelian. With the fall of Zenobia's Palmyrene Empire, Rome was able to secure the eastern provinces again.

The only part of the Roman Empire left for Aurelian to reconquer was Britannia and Gaul—both of which were still under the Gallic Empire. Wishing to avoid more bloodshed, the emperor resorted to diplomacy, an attempt that failed. He was forced to lay an attack on the empire. The Battle of Châlons took place in 274 and was won by Aurelian's forces. Sources claim that Aurelian lost six thousand men, while Tetricus I, the emperor of the Gallic Empire at the time, lost nearly fifty thousand. After thirteen years of independence, the Gallic Empire finally collapsed, and its provinces were returned to the Romans.

Despite Aurelian's success in restoring the empire, he did not end the Third Century Crisis, although he set in motion the events that led to its end. After Aurelian's death, six more emperors rose to the throne and continued to help the empire solve the ongoing crisis. It was not until the reign of Diocletian that Rome finally began to see the light at the end of the tunnel. Although Diocletian's reign was filled with warfare and violence, the emperor brought glory back to the Roman Empire and ended Rome's fifty-year-long turmoil with his carefully planned strategies and reforms.

Chapter 5 – From the Tetrarchy to the Fall of the West

It was the year 285 CE, and the people of Rome had gathered around to celebrate the return of Diocletian, their emperor who had just emerged victorious from the Battle of the Margus. Some might have assumed that Diocletian was no different from any other emperor before him and that it was nearly impossible for the empire to rise after suffering from the fifty-year-long crisis. After all, Diocletian came from a rather humble background, despite having vast experience in the military. However, his intelligence and reforms finally dragged Rome out of its misery.

From Diocletian's point of view, he saw the empire as too big. One man could not oversee every single matter. Two men should be put in charge to ensure the empire was at its best. So, Diocletian decided to call upon his close friend he had known from his days in the military. His name was Maximian. Diocletian made him his co-emperor, bestowing him the title of Caesar. Not long after that, he gave him the most honorable Roman title: Augustus. With two emperors on the throne, Diocletian split the empire into two: East and West. While Diocletian chose to oversee matters in the East, Maximian was put in charge of ruling over the West. Nicomedia (an ancient city once located in modern-day Turkey) was made the capital of the Eastern Roman Empire. Maximian chose the city of Milan as the capital of the Western Roman Empire.

Diocletian began securing the East from future threats, meeting little to no obstacles. He made peace with the Persians and secured alliances with the Arab tribes that had once acted against the empire. However, Maximian faced a different situation. A self-proclaimed emperor in Britain threatened his position. He worked on eliminating the threat by launching an attack on Britain, which proved challenging, especially when Germanic tribes invaded the western provinces. Diocletian soon journeyed to the West, and the two emperors joined forces to push back the barbarians and put the other threats to rest.

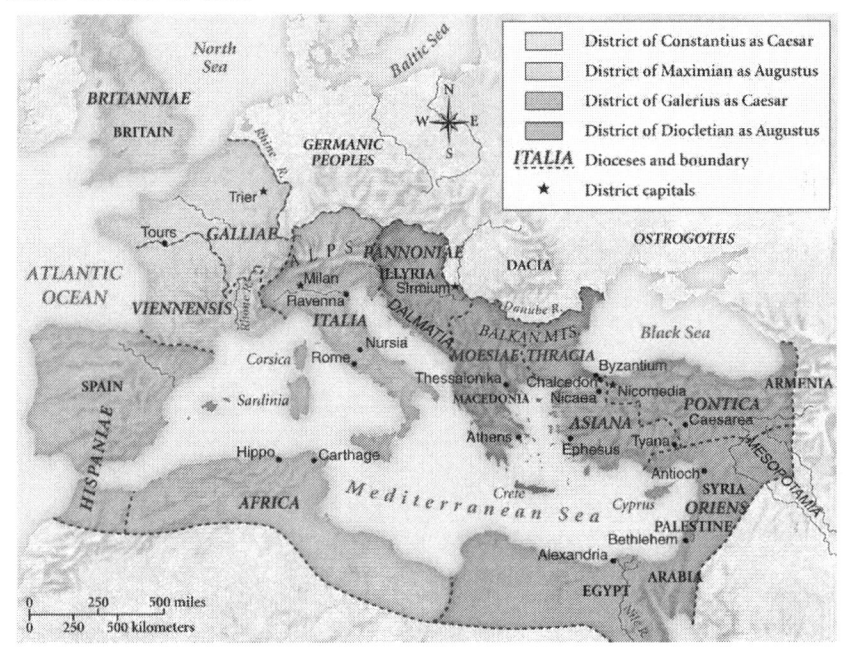

Map of the Roman Empire under the Tetrarchy.
Coppermine Photo Gallery, CC BY-SA 3.0 <http://creativecommons.org/licenses/by-sa/3.0/>, via Wikimedia Commons: https://commons.wikimedia.org/wiki/File:Tetrarchy_map3.jpg

After witnessing multiple invasions and other problems, the emperors came to the conclusion that they needed more assistance. Diocletian suggested they appoint one emperor each who would rule under their supervision. Diocletian's chose a man named Galerius, while Maximian appointed Constantius—both of these men were the prefects of their Praetorian Guard. The two men were given the title Caesar (junior emperor) and would rule alongside their respective Augustus (senior emperor). Four emperors now controlled the vast Roman Empire. This reform is known to historians as the Tetrarchy, and as much as it brought the Roman Empire back to its feet, it would also cause troubles as the years passed.

How the Tetrarchy Began to Crumble

With the abdication of Diocletian and Maximian in 305, the empire's leadership was put on the shoulders of their Caesars, who were promoted to the rank of Augustus. Galerius ruled over the East with his newly appointed Caesar, Maximinus, while the West was put under the control of Constantius and his subordinate, Severus. However, the appointments of the new Caesars were not accepted by all, especially Maxentius (the son of Maximian) and Constantine (the son of Constantius), both of whom were initially seen as the next in line. It did not take long for the empire to witness another succession issue.

In 306, the Augustus of the West, Constantius, marched to Britain to lead a campaign against the Picts. Unfortunately, he succumbed to leukemia the same year, leaving his throne open for a new capable leader to claim. His Caesar, Severus, was quickly named the new Augustus. However, this was not acknowledged by Constantius's army, who hailed the late emperor's son, Constantine, as the ruler of the West (some sources claim Constantius named his son the next Augustus). To calm the strained succession issue, Galerius officially named Constantine Caesar instead.

Another matter arose the following year. Maxentius, who had earned the support of the Praetorian Guard and the people of Rome, proclaimed himself emperor. Since no one acknowledged his self-proclaimed power, all four emperors of the Tetrarchy planned to remove him. In 307, Severus marched to Rome with his troops, hoping to put an end to Maxentius, but the defection of his army forced him to retreat. He was soon captured and murdered. As Maxentius's army grew, he resumed his unofficial rule over Italy alongside his father, Maximian, who had resurfaced from his retirement a few years earlier. Sometime in the same year, Galerius attacked them to no avail; his army also defected to Maxentius's side.

Following the advice of the retired Diocletian, the emperors chose another man to replace the now-dead Severus. The Tetrarchy saw the arrival of Valerius Licinianus Licinius, the new Augustus of the West, while Constantine remained his Caesar. Maximian still craved power and attempted to overthrow Constantine, which failed and led to his demise. Galerius, on the other hand, died after battling a horrible disease, possibly bowel cancer or gangrene. His death was rejoiced by the Christians, as it meant the end of their ruthless persecutions.

Wars among the emperors raged for years to come. Constantine exploited Maxentius's weakness when he lost support from the citizens of Rome by launching an attack and invading Italy. The night before the battle, Constantine was believed to have had a dream of Jesus Christ. He ordered his troops to march into battle with the Christian cross on their shields and banners. His victory against Maxentius at the Battle of the Milvian Bridge allowed him to gain complete control of the West.

Constantine shifted his focus to Licinius, who had successfully seized control of the East following Maximinus's defeat. The two fought multiple times before Licinius finally surrendered in 324. After crushing the Tetrarchy and reuniting the empire, Constantine became the sole emperor.

An illustration of Constantine leading his army against Maxentius at the Milvian Bridge.
https://commons.wikimedia.org/wiki/File:Battle_of_the_Milvian_Bridge_by_Giulio_Romano,_1520-24.jpg

Constantine, the First Christian Emperor of Rome

As the sole emperor of Rome, Constantine was free to rule over the vast empire as he pleased without facing any threats or disagreements from other Roman rulers. After seeing the decaying state of Rome, the emperor sought out a new location for his capital. He first thought of the site of the ancient city of Troy but changed his mind. Nicomedia was not on his radar since it once belonged to Diocletian; Constantine wanted a place untouched by previous emperors. So, he chose the ancient city of Byzantium. Its strategic location and great harbor made it the perfect choice.

Constantine began working on his new capital. He invited artisans throughout the empire to rebuild the city and used the rich resources obtained from the provinces. Walls were built, and avenues were constructed, along with several statues of powerful figures of Roman history, including himself. Constantine even commissioned the construction of Christian churches, cisterns, and pagan temples in his new capital. By 330, Byzantium, renamed Constantinople, was exactly how he had envisioned it.

After experiencing a dream of Jesus Christ in 312, right before his big battle, Constantine was said to have converted to Christianity; some sources, however, claim he was baptized on his deathbed. Nonetheless, the great emperor showed signs of his devotion. As soon as Constantine acquired the throne, he immediately sent his mother, a devoted Christian, on a pilgrimage, which resulted in the construction of the Church of the Nativity at Bethlehem. Gladiatorial games ended since killing for entertainment was against the beliefs of Christianity. Pagan sacrificial rituals also ended.

Constantine's best-known contribution to the Christians was the Edict of Milan, which was established in 313, before the war with Licinius. Since Christianity was functionally illegal in the Roman Empire at the beginning of the religion's existence, many Christians had perished due to persecution. Emperor Nero blamed the Christians for the terrible Great Fire, leading to many of their deaths. Even Diocletian passed a decree allowing for the official persecution of Christians in 303. Although Constantine was not the first to legalize Christianity, his edict was effective. The Edict of

Milan officially declared the abolishment of the persecution of Christians while protecting the rights of Christian citizens. Those arrested were released from prison, and their confiscated properties were returned. The edict also declared tolerance for all faiths. Even though Christianity did not become the empire's official religion—this happened during the reign of Emperor Theodosius in 380 — Constantine no doubt contributed to the spread of the religion.

During the years of his blossoming reign, the great emperor remained a military commander and had dozens of successes defending his empire against foreign threats. With his son, Constantius II, by his side, he defeated several barbarian tribes on the battlefield and reconquered the territories once lost to the Dacians. He planned to capture Persia, but his illness prevented him from doing so. He died in 337 after ruling over the reunited empire for over thirty years.

From glory and stability, the empire was again thrown into another set of skirmishes after the passing of Constantine. Power struggles between his family members were brewing, and they all fought for the throne. However, in the end, Constantine's three sons rose to power after eliminating their rivals.

With one matter resolved, another arose; the empire was facing constant trouble, with wars and rebellions happening almost weekly. While trying to return stability and peace to the empire, two of Constantine's ruling sons perished, leaving Constantius II as the sole emperor. Seeing all the ongoing issues in the empire, Constantius II decided to appoint a co-emperor to rule the West. His cousin, Julian, was chosen, who would soon prove to be a highly efficient ruler. Threatened by Julian's success, Constantius II aimed to bring down his own appointed co-emperor. However, he died of an illness before their battle, thus leaving Julian as the only ruler.

In addition to his military successes, Julian was also known for his effort to revive paganism. He even reversed some of the Edict of Milan that had restrained pagan practices. The emperor, also known as Julian the Apostate to the Christians, faced his demise during his campaign against the Sassanid forces. He died due to a spear wound. The battle with the Sassanids was only the beginning, as peace and glory were no longer on the horizon for the Roman

Empire.

The Fall of the West

The empire soon sensed even bigger troubles when they saw the beginning of the Germanic tribes' migration. The extreme pressure from the powerful Huns had caused these barbarians to seek refuge within the empire; some entered peacefully, while others did not. The Visigoth, for instance, approached the frontiers of the empire by 376, hoping for a safe refuge. They were welcomed by the ruling emperor, Valens, with the condition that they defend the borders from any threats. However, the situation quickly went south, as the Romans failed to accommodate the large tribe—it was estimated that there were nearly eighty thousand of them. Combined with the hostility portrayed by most of the Romans toward them, the Visigoths rebelled, which led to a bloodbath called the Battle of Adrianople.

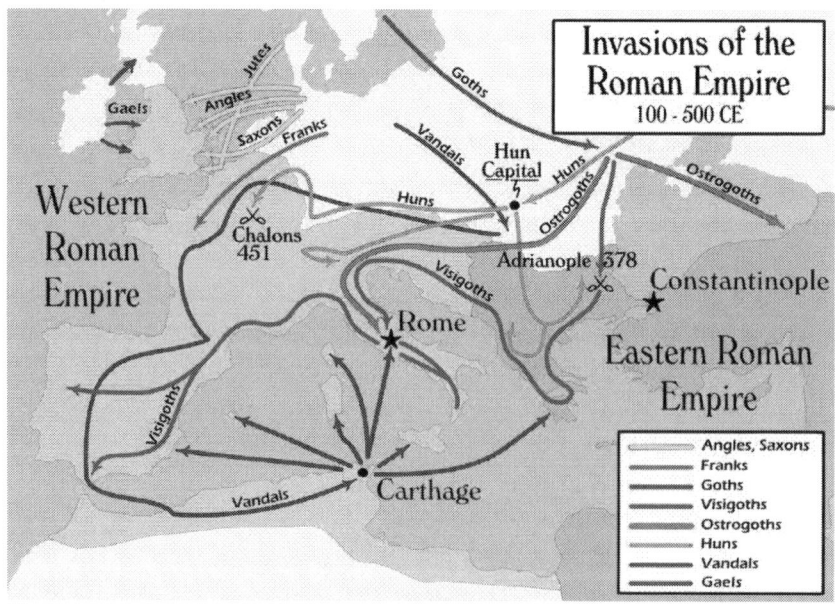

Routes taken by barbarian invaders of the Roman Empire during the Migration Period.
User:MapMaster, CC BY-SA 2.5 <https://creativecommons.org/licenses/by-sa/2.5>, via Wikimedia Commons: https://commons.wikimedia.org/wiki/File:Invasions_of_the_Roman_Empire_1.png

The large Roman infantry was headed by Valens, while the Germanic Visigoths were led by Fritigern. The Visigoths were also aided by the Ostrogoths. On August 9th, 378, the battle began with an attack launched by a few Roman commanders. Since the assault was launched without an order, the rest of the troops were confused, which opened an opportunity for the Ostrogothic cavalry to charge from the mountains and annihilate the Roman infantry. Over forty thousand Romans were killed, including Valens. With the emperor's body lying lifeless on the battlefield, the barbarians emerged victorious, although it was only for a short while. They were soon pushed back to Thrace by the Roman army, which was led by the next emperor, Theodosius.

A 19th-century painting possibly depicting the sacking of Rome.
https://commons.wikimedia.org/wiki/File:Cole_Thomas_The_Course_of_Empire_Destruction_1836.jpg

Theodosius successfully ran campaigns against the Goths and suppressed two civil wars during his sixteen years on the throne. But the Roman Empire was far from achieving peace, as it was split into two again in 395. It was passed to Theodosius's two sons: Arcadius and Honorius. Since the well-fortified Eastern Roman Empire remained impenetrable, many aggressors shifted their focus to the West. In 410, the Visigoths, under the leadership of King Alaric, launched an attack on Rome. The old, decaying city, which was once the most glorious part of the empire, was beyond saving. It received no help from the East. The great city of Rome was sacked, marking the beginning of the end of the Western Roman Empire.

Decades after the fall of Rome, the Western Roman Empire was forced into another ferocious battle. This time, it was against the great army led by Attila the Hun. Attila had been rampaging all over the empire, causing extreme fear. His advance was put to a halt by Flavius Aetius, a brilliant Roman commander.

Acknowledging the Huns as extremely formidable warriors, the Roman commander resorted to unlikely allies—the Visigoths, Franks, Burgundians, and Alans. After forming alliances with these Germanic tribes, Aetius led his entire army to the Catalaunian Plains (located in modern-day Champagne, France), where he would clash swords with Attila and his fierce warriors. Making use of his past experiences on the battlefield, Aetius successfully defeated Attila, who was forced to withdraw from the war.

The Battle of the Catalaunian Plains was indeed a great success for Aetius, but it was not enough to bring the Western Roman Empire back to its glory. The death of Attila the following year was seen as good news for the Romans, for without his leadership, the Hunnic Empire would not thrive, thus saving the empire from further threats. However, the Germanic tribes never stopped their conquests of the Western Roman Empire. In 476, the Germanic soldier Odoacer managed to overthrow the young emperor, Romulus Augustulus, and claimed the title of the first king of Italy. While the East remained strong, later on becoming the Byzantine Empire, the disposal of the last Western emperor marked the end of the Western Roman Empire.

Chapter 6 – Trade and Transportation

The Roman Empire might have gone down in history for its flourishing wealth, economy, architecture, art, warfare, and successful conquests. But many are not aware that the vast empire was also known for its long stretches of road networks, some of which still exist today. Of course, roads were not invented by the Romans; the first road was constructed by the early Mesopotamian civilizations. The Romans borrowed the idea and expanded the concept, mostly for military reasons. The first ever *via* or Roman road is known as the Via Appia, more popularly referred to as the Appian Way.

An illustration of the Appian Way.
https://commons.wikimedia.org/wiki/File:Antichina_piranese.jpg

Parts of the Appian Way that survived the centuries.
https://commons.wikimedia.org/wiki/File:Minturno_Via-Appia.jpg

Constructed in 312 BCE, this ancient road was commissioned by Appius Claudius Caecus, a brilliant statesman who served the Roman Republic as a censor or magistrate. The road initially ran for over 200 kilometers (about 125 miles), beginning in Rome and ending in the ancient city of Capua in Campania. Almost seven decades later, the road was extended for another three hundred kilometers (nearly two hundred miles) to Brundisium, which was located along the Adriatic Sea. Back then, it was common for Roman roads to be built as straight as possible. The first ninety kilometers (fifty-five miles) of the Appian Way, for instance, was constructed in a straight line until it reached Terracina, a city situated on the coast of the Tyrrhenian Sea. From there, the road took its first turn and was built inland to reach Capua. Later on, more road networks were established, mainly to ease the movements of the military. The Roman Empire was believed to have had a total of 372 roads that connected over a hundred of its provinces. Out of the 400,000 kilometers (about 250,000 miles) of roadways, more than 80,000 kilometers (50,000 miles) were stone-paved highways.

The process of building these roads was a difficult task, especially since they were expected to last for centuries. Since the Romans preferred their roads to be built in a straight line, surveys had to be conducted to determine the correct engineering methods. They would scout the route where the road was supposed to run and observe any natural obstacles in the way. They would cut down forests, drain lakes and marshes, divert creeks, and cut through mountainsides just so the roads could be constructed without turns. Arched bridges were built to cross heavy streams, while tunnels were used to cut through mountains and avoid lengthy detours.

The Roman roads were one of the empire's greatest architectural achievements. Many agree that these road networks were the arteries of the empire and the main key to its impressive might. Other than being used by legionnaires to march toward a captured city and perhaps outmaneuver their enemies, the road system also allowed Roman civilians to travel across the provinces in just a matter of days to visit family members or conduct trade or business. Supplies, emergency help, and reinforcements could easily reach even the most isolated parts of the empire since the roads were specifically designed with speed in mind.

The first emperor of Rome, Augustus, made the decision to establish the *cursus publicus*, the very first courier service in the empire. Historians believe that the establishment of *cursus publicus* was influenced by the Persians. These messengers were put in charge of delivering different types of messages, be they from high officials or senators or even tax revenues from provinces at the end of the western frontier.

Most of the time, the messengers would ride on a horse; sources state it could be plausible that they rode an average of eighty kilometers (fifty miles) a day. The strategic road network no doubt shortened the amount of time needed for the couriers to reach their destination. From Rome, it took roughly seven and a half days to reach the Gallo-Roman town of Lutetia (modern-day Paris). The task of a messenger might have sounded decent, but it was often a dangerous job. Since couriers carried valuable supplies and important mail, they were often targeted by thieves.

The messengers would also travel across the provinces in a light carriage pulled by a couple of fast horses. A birota, a slow, two-wheeled cart pulled by oxen, was used, though it was strictly reserved for delivering official government letters and documents. Since the wheels of Roman carriages were made out of iron, loud and unpleasant sounds were often produced whenever they passed by. Roman law strictly prohibited any kind of carriage from entering the cities during the day.

At every twenty-five kilometers along the Roman roads, one could find a *mansio*. Directly translated as "staying place," a *mansio* was a way station. They were normally commissioned by the government to act as a resting spot for couriers and travelers. Starting off as a simple structure that served drinks and sometimes food, the area surrounding a *mansio* would often attract many other businesses, resulting in the emergence of small towns. Although military camps were a common sight near *mansiones*, some suggest that these resting areas had a rather bad reputation due to the frequent visits of prostitutes and criminals.

The Different Types of Roman Transportation

While *biga*, the two-horse chariot, was often used in races and various ceremonies, the Romans used another type of swift chariot called *essedum* to traverse cities. A much slower version of this was a *cisium*. Unlike the *essedum*, the *cisium* featured a seat for two passengers.

A bronze figurine of a *biga* from Roman Gaul.
https://commons.wikimedia.org/wiki/File:Bige_Mus%C3%A9e_de_Laon_050208.jpg

For longer journeys, Roman citizens would opt for a *raeda*, a Roman wagon that could trace its roots to the Celts. Almost equivalent to modern-day buses, some of these ancient carriages had cloth roofs to protect passengers from the weather, although those without coverings were pretty common. Inside, the wagon had several benches that could fit multiple passengers. Even though there was a space to place supplies and luggage, the Roman law set a maximum weight limit; each carriage was only allowed to carry less than a thousand Roman *libra* (about 330 kilograms or 730 pounds) of luggage. When a *raeda* was not drawn by four healthy horses, oxen and mules were used to pull the carriage.

The wealthy would travel short distances on a litter, which was carried by six bearers or slaves. This mode of transportation was especially popular among wealthy women since it was a safer option when traveling the city streets. While middle-class Romans used *raeda* to travel in groups, the wealthy rode in a *carpentum*, which was more comfortable than the simple carriage. Not only was it entirely covered with an arched wooden roof, but it was also adequately adorned and spacious. A smaller version of a *carpentum* was known as *carruca*, which could only fit two passengers.

A Roman *carruca*, which was often used by the rich.
https://commons.wikimedia.org/wiki/File:Carruca.jpg

An illustration of a *plaustrum* carrying heavy items.
https://commons.wikimedia.org/wiki/File:PSM_V18_D470_Ancient_roman_farm_kart_and_oxen.jpg

Plaustrum, an open wagon pulled by oxen, was also a common sight. Made entirely out of wood and two to four solid iron-shod wheels, this particular form of transportation was used to transport heavy goods. Construction materials, such as bricks and stones, along with agricultural goods, including olive oil, grapes, wines, cereals, and grains, were some of the items this wagon carried.

How the Roman Empire Gained the Majority of Its Revenue from Egypt

The Eternal City had always been interested in Egypt due to the vast wealth held by the Ptolemaic rulers. When two of Rome's most influential rulers, Augustus and Mark Antony, agreed on an alliance and formed the Second Triumvirate, the two split their powers, with Antony securing the rule over the East, including precious Egypt. There, he formed an alliance with Egypt's queen, Cleopatra VII, who was also a descendant of Ptolemy, one of the four generals who served under Alexander the Great. With Cleopatra by his side and her wealth within reach, the Roman general planned to launch a campaign against the Parthian Empire—an ambition that seriously damaged Egypt's economy. Despite the region's gradual decline, Antony set his eyes on war campaigns instead of restoring Egypt's decaying infrastructure. The canals, for instance, were completely neglected, which disrupted Egypt's irrigation and transportation systems.

Despite the province's gradual decline, Augustus managed to obtain most, if not all, of the treasures that once belonged to the Ptolemaic rulers, including the valuable religious offerings gathered by Cleopatra. However, instead of putting this great fortune in his personal coffers, the young emperor used it on his people; Roman citizens were said to have received nearly four hundred sesterces each, while the military was showered with generous gifts. This move not only guaranteed the emperor's popularity among his subjects but also played a profound role in the empire's economy. The Roman Empire began to witness a consumer boom, which soon led to increased prices on all types of goods, thus attracting more foreign merchants and traders to Rome.

Seeing that the Eternal City was beginning to welcome an increasing number of merchants from outside the empire, Augustus turned his attention to the Egyptian Red Sea ports and its sea lanes. He began restoring Egypt to its former glory, ordering several construction projects across the once-neglected land. Due to these rapid restorations, Egypt was able to resume its flourishing agricultural activities. Roads and trade routes were also greatly improved under the emperor's supervision, with caravan stations built along the way to grant the traveling merchants some respite. Military outposts and watchtowers were installed to ensure smooth communication and safety. At times, merchants who carried extra precious cargo were given the convenience of an escort by the Roman army. The emperor also paid attention to the several harbor cities along the Nile, especially the city of Coptos, which was considered the main hub for receiving exotic goods imported from Arabia, India, and Africa.

These restoration efforts, combined with the Roman administration, no doubt impacted the empire's import and export industries. With the growing number of ships beginning to sail out of Egypt to as far as India, the empire was able to gain attractive revenue from import taxes. One ship known as the *Hermapollon* was said to have returned to Egypt from India with exotic spices and goods worth at least nine million sesterces. From this ship alone, the empire collected 25 percent on tax, which was equivalent to approximately two million sesterces. Records claim the empire collected about 250 million sesterces per year through import taxes and another 25 million sesterces per annum through export taxes.

Under the reign of Augustus, Egypt alone contributed to almost half of the empire's income. The revenue produced by the province continued to grow as the years passed. By the mid-1st century CE, Egypt produced at least six million sesterces per annum, which made up two-thirds of the imperial coffer.

Trade Goods in Imperial Rome

While Egypt was the main entry point for goods originating from the Far East, the Western Roman Empire had Ostia as its main port, as it was located closest to Rome. Its location right at the mouth of the Tiber River made it possible for imported goods to arrive in the Eternal City in just a matter of days. Since transporting goods via the roads was rather expensive, merchants and traders preferred to travel the seas, although it was riskier given the unpredictability of the weather and sea conditions. Because of this, the Romans did their best to ensure the sea routes were safe. Several lighthouses were built, and the Roman navy was deployed to clear out any pirates sailing the waters.

The Romans did not only import goods internationally; they also received goods from their own provinces. Britannia, for instance, supplied Rome with wool, tin, lead, and silver, which they often used to craft jewelry and mint coins. The provinces in the East, on the other hand, provided color dyes for clothing, along with cotton, perfumes, and spices. Grains arrived in the Eternal City from North Africa, which also provided wild animals that were typically used in gladiatorial games. Different types of food and consumables were common trade goods among the Roman provinces, such as the fish sauce garum, olive oil, cereals, and, of course, wine, which was considered an important part of the Roman diet. Internationally, Rome was known to have exported a variety of goods to different parts of the globe, with grapes, pottery, and papyrus being some examples.

The Romans loved wearing silk, especially those in the upper class—though, according to the historian Marcellinus Ammianus, garments made out of silk began to be worn by almost every social class by the late 4th century CE. The Romans were greatly pleased when they finally made direct contact with China in 166 CE. From there on, silk became a common sight in the empire, as the Romans began to welcome imports from China through the Silk Road. In regards to India, Rome was believed to have imported over a hundred items, including exotic spices, sandalwood, glass beads, ivory, and even peacocks. Slaves were also imported into Rome from regions and kingdoms outside of the empire.

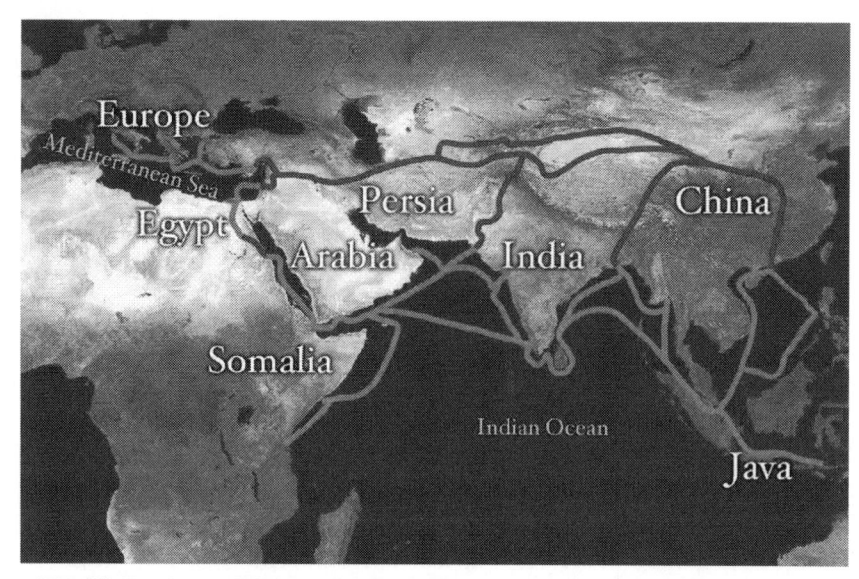

The Silk Road was used for trading goods. The land routes are shown in red, and the maritime routes are in blue.
https://commons.wikimedia.org/wiki/File:Silk_route.jpg

Trade and commerce in the Roman empire lasted for centuries and kept Rome financially stable. It was only when the Goths captured Ostia that its trade economy started to plummet. Without the control of the harbor, the Romans were unable to import grains and other food supplies, leading to mass starvation—which was the key to the Goths' victory. When the Western Roman Empire collapsed, the Mediterranean was yet again surrounded by dangers, blocking many merchants and traders from conducting business in the Eternal City.

Chapter 7 – Central and Provincial Governing

Somewhere within the safe walls of the Eternal City, a man could be seen rushing his way through the bustling crowds in the ancient Forum. He was probably nearing his fifties and wearing a toga with a broad Tyrian purple stripe: a symbol of high status. On one of his fingers was a special golden ring, a sign that the man indeed belonged to the higher social class of Rome. The man finally arrived at his destination, the Curia Julia, one of the most prominent structures in ancient Rome, commissioned by the great Julius Caesar and completed by Augustus himself. The man continued his pace and entered the Senate house. He then proceeded to take his seat among his fellow senators and got ready for a meeting where they would discuss Rome's next leader.

Roman senators discussing state matters.
https://commons.wikimedia.org/wiki/File:Cicer%C3%B3n_denuncia_a_Catilina,_por_Cesare_Maccari.jpg

Before Augustus gained victory over Mark Antony at Actium, Rome was basically put under the control of the Senate. According to Roman tradition, the birth of the Senate could be traced back to when the Eternal City was first founded. Its first legendary king, Romulus, was the one responsible for the establishment of the Senate. It was believed that Romulus had handpicked a hundred of his best men as the first senators. They were entrusted with a simple task: to provide advice to the sovereign. Although records of how crucial the Senate played a part back then are rather vague, historians agree that the Senate began to grow in power when the Roman monarchy was nearing its end.

Rome became a republic when the seventh king of Rome, Lucius Tarquinius Superbus, was finally overthrown. The absence of a crown on top of the hierarchy paved the way for the Senate to rise and expand its power. Beginning with only a hundred men, the number of senators increased to six hundred. It then grew to nine hundred under the order of Caesar but decreased back to six hundred when Augustus took the reins. Although placed at the top of the social classes, being a senator was not a walk in the park. First and foremost, to become a part of the Senate, one had to be wealthy enough, as senators were not paid any salary and were strictly prohibited from getting involved in commerce and trade. In fact, they were expected to fund the state. Once appointed, senators would serve until their dying breath. If they were caught in a dishonorable act or if their wealth was depleted for some reason, the senator must resign.

During the early period of the republic, the Senate was mainly responsible for advising the magistrates, such as censors and consuls. The senators had no power to pass laws; they could only suggest decrees to the magistrates. After a formal discussion and gaining votes, decrees became laws and were implemented throughout the state. However, by the 4th century BCE, the Senate's authority grew. It was in charge of almost every aspect of the government, including religious matters. Not only was the Senate put in charge of the city's money flow, but it was also powerful enough to appoint favored officials to govern a certain province or promote someone to the rank of *legatus* or general. The senators also had the authority to declare war against their enemies; Julius Caesar and Mark Antony were once branded as public enemies. During desperate times, they could also appoint someone—typically one who had an exceptional background in the military—as dictator.

The Senate was no doubt the most powerful official body in Rome for centuries. After the rise of Rome's first emperor, Augustus, the Senate saw its power gradually wane. During the early imperial period, the Senate still held a considerable amount of influence within the empire; senators were allowed to debate and disagree with the emperor's decisions. They retained some of their authority, both in the military and over religious matters. The Senate was also allowed to appoint governors but only for certain provinces—typically those that were not put under the direct watch of Augustus. The court of law was handled by the senators, and their rulings were final—not even the emperor could overturn them.

However, as time went by, the Senate continued to face various threats to its power and prestige, especially when the military began to gain the upper hand at the start of the Third Century Crisis. The Senate finally lost most of its authority when the emperor's official seat was moved to the East. Although the Roman Senate was split into two bodies—one remained in the crumbling Rome while the other in Constantinople—they were involved only in minor and local matters.

The Roman Emperor, a Man Who Held True Power over the Empire

Even though the early days of the empire retained the Roman Republic's political structure, the Senate's powers were in name only, especially after the reign of Augustus. At this point, the Senate existed only to endorse the emperor's decisions. If the senators refused, they could face serious punishments, including death.

The ruling emperor had complete control over the empire's coffers; they could spend any sum of money on anything they wished, be it the construction of a new temple or even a statue depicting their likeness. Their words were also final. Nero, who was described by many as an emperor who was always in need of money, freely pointed his fingers toward those he disliked, saying they were involved in a certain conspiracy. The person would get arrested and often be murdered. His wealth would be confiscated and given to the emperor. Nero often used this method to fund his expensive construction projects.

The emperor also had control of the majority of the military. Augustus himself was the commander of twenty-six legions, which comprised approximately 125,000 highly trained soldiers. None could run for office without the emperor's approval. The emperor was very involved, even in the city's religious affairs. Augustus and the emperors after him assumed the title of Pontifex Maximus or "Chief Priest," signifying that he had the ultimate authority over every religious ceremony.

The provincial governors were put under close supervision, and the emperor was allowed to call upon his people for assembly should he feel the need to enact new laws. In short, the emperor was the only man who held true power over the vast empire to the point that, even after their deaths, some were deified—a religious tradition the Romans possibly assimilated from the East.

How the Roman Provinces Were Governed

The empire's rapid expansion made it impossible for the emperor to oversee every matter across the hundreds of provinces. During the republic, each of the provinces was put under the watch of a Roman magistrate appointed by the Senate. They would rule over the provinces while being supported by a quaestor, a lower-ranking magistrate whose main responsibility was the treasury, along with three lieutenants. However, extortion and abuses were common in these Roman provinces, as the governors were given complete control.

During the early Roman Empire, reforms for the provincial governments were introduced. Procurators were appointed to curb extortion issues and financial mismanagement. Governors were chosen among either consuls or praetors, who would then draw lots to determine which provinces they would assume control over. The governors then had to issue the *lex provinciae*, sets of laws to help the administration of the provinces.

After Augustus rose to power, the provinces were split into two different classes. While the senatorial provinces were still governed by appointed consuls and praetors, the imperial provinces were put under the control of propraetorian legates, who were the ruling emperor's representatives. Although the provinces were overseen by different types of governors, Augustus set a general governing policy to lessen corruption and unjust administration.

As governors, they had four main responsibilities. Since they were in charge of a province's taxes and financial matters, they were expected to oversee every single local authority and private tax collector. Their second duty was to supervise all construction projects and ensure the flow of money was in line with the projects. Other than paying close attention to the province's financial situation, a governor also carried the responsibility of a supreme judge. They had the power to impose death penalties. While major provinces across the empire had more than one legion ready for battles, smaller provinces typically consisted of auxiliaries. Nevertheless, governors were the ones expected to command the army if there were any threats.

How the Military Asserted Their Power in Imperial Rome

As time passed, the six hundred senators were no longer considered serious contenders to the imperial throne, as their power slowly diminished. However, as the vast empire continued to grow, expanding its borders farther to the east and west, emperors began to rely on the military. Without them, the empire would fall into pieces in no time, especially since the empire had made a lot of enemies as the years progressed. The imperial government was left with little choice but to ensure the military remained loyal to the emperor. They showered the military with gifts, attractive salaries, prestigious awards, and many other promises, hoping they would never turn their backs on the ruling emperor and continue to protect the empire's frontiers from any impending foreign threats.

However, the military quickly noticed how their emperor held a slight fear of them. Many emperors who had just risen to the throne resorted to buying the military's loyalty, but sometimes, the promised payments never arrived, which led the military to take matters into its own hands. Rebellions, threats, and even assassinations were carried out by the military whenever the imperial government showed signs of negligence. These violent episodes of bloodshed, mutinies, and killings were common, especially during the Third Century Crisis.

Out of all the military classes, historians believe the Praetorian Guard was the empire's third power player. Although the Praetorian Guard was said to have been established shortly after Rome transformed into an empire, this elite military unit traces its origins back to the Roman Republic. Back then, the Praetorian Guard was mainly responsible for providing escorts to high-ranking officials of the Senate and the Roman legions. It was only during the beginning of Augustus's reign in 27 BCE that the Praetorian Guard saw some changes. Instead of providing security to elite officials, the Praetorian Guard was tasked with keeping the emperor and his family safe.

A relief of the Praetorian Guard.
Historien spécialiste du bassin minier du Nord-Pas-de-Calais JÄNNICK Jérémy / Wikimedia Commons & Louvre-Lens: https://commons.wikimedia.org/wiki/File:Lens_-_Inauguration_du_Louvre-Lens_le_4_d%C3%A9cembre_2012,_la_Galerie_du_Temps,_n%C2%B0_058.JPG

The number of men in the Praetorian Guard varied as the years went by. It began with a total of 4,500 handpicked soldiers during the reign of Rome's first emperor and grew to 15,000 by the late empire. This elite unit lived in special barracks referred to as Castra Praetoria, which was said to be right on the outskirts of Rome. The salary of the Praetorians was rather lucrative; they earned about three times more than a regular soldier. They were also entitled to *donativum*, a form of gift money worth several years of pay each time a new emperor took the reins. The highest rank within this special elite force was called a Praetorian prefect, and some of them were known for playing major roles in the harsh political sphere.

As part of protecting the ruling emperor, the Praetorian Guard had to act as anti-riot forces, secret police, and sometimes fire brigades. They often went undercover, dressing as normal citizens and eavesdropping on suspicious conversations, especially at gladiatorial games and theatrical performances. Those who showed even the tiniest signs of treason would be arrested and interrogated. The Praetorians even secretly assassinated those who they deemed an imminent threat to the government and emperor. The Praetorians performed their duty well during the first few decades of the Roman Empire. However, with Augustus's passing and the rise of Tiberius, the Praetorian Guard began to show its true colors.

The first prefect who successfully elevated the involvement of the Praetorian Guard in Rome's political sphere was Sejanus. Many agree that Sejanus was a highly ambitious man whose ultimate goal was to secure the entire empire. In fact, he briefly realized his dreams when the state's matters were left to his judgment after he successfully persuaded Tiberius to leave the imperial seat and reside in his luxurious mansion away from Rome. However, in the end, Sejanus's own greed and thirst for power sealed his fate.

Although Tiberius never left the prefect as the de facto ruler of Rome, Sejanus began to gain political influence, especially from his loyal comrades. The Senate eventually grew fond of him but only for a short while, as he was quick to abuse his power. Treason trials were brought back, and many perished due to his greed. At this point, the government was in shambles, and the people of Rome lived in fear. Sejanus shifted his focus to Drusus, Tiberius's only son and heir apparent to the imperial throne. With the help of Livilla, the wife of Drusus, whom Sejanus had managed to seduce, Sejanus poisoned the only son of Tiberius, thus eliminating the emperor's heir. (It should be noted that scholars aren't entirely certain whether Sejanus did this, but it is likely.)

Sejanus arrested and condemned to death.
https://commons.wikimedia.org/wiki/File:Sejanus_is_arrested_and_condemned_to_death.jpg

To make himself a legitimate heir to the throne, Sejanus attempted to marry Livilla, although this move was denied by Tiberius. The emperor soon learned of Sejanus's true intentions and, with careful planning, managed to execute the ambitious prefect. Due to Sejanus's troublesome rule, the Senate immediately ordered *damnatio memoriae* or condemnation of memory. All of Sejanus's actions and previous achievements might have been excluded from official Roman accounts, but his influence remained within the Praetorian Guard. The Praetorians' power grew tremendously after their success in assassinating Caligula. They not only had the power to eliminate emperors—the Praetorians were famously known for killing thirteen Roman emperors throughout the centuries—but could also select the next ruling emperor.

Although the Praetorians began as an elite military unit with a noble cause, they turned power-hungry and became feared and despised by many, including the emperors. In the 4th century CE, the Praetorian Guard's terror finally ended. After a long series of treasonous actions, Emperor Constantine decided the Praetorian Guard could no longer be trusted, resulting in their permanent disbandment.

Chapter 8 – Imperial Army and Warfare

Farmers, merchants, fishermen, artisans, bakers, and blacksmiths—these were some of the most common occupations that existed in the Roman Empire. Indeed, one could be free from any life-endangering situations should they choose any of these career paths since their jobs were often conducted within the safety of fortified walls, but not all of these professions promised great fortune. Farmers could plant more than a hundred different crops each year, but their chances of owning their own land were slim; bakers could sell dozens of loaves and other goods, but it was nearly impossible for them to move out of their dilapidated high-rise apartments and into a landed house with paved streets and guaranteed security. Back then, fortune and wealth were enough to push Roman citizens into enlisting in the military—one of the few occupations with steady pay.

Being one of the biggest and most powerful empires at the time, it is not surprising that the Roman Empire gathered its fair share of enemies whose sole ambition was to dethrone the reigning emperor and claim every one of his vast regions. Even ancient historians agreed that the empire was synonymous with warfare almost all the time. Because of that, the empire always welcomed recruits who were headstrong in lending the emperor their ultimate loyalty and sword. As much as the Romans would like to defend their empire from foreign forces, they chose to devote themselves to the military because of the lucrative rewards that came with it. Retired soldiers were promised land of their own and a lifetime pension—that is, if they survived the many battles and had served the empire for twenty-five years.

Those interested in joining the military had to fulfill several requirements before raising their swords on the battlefield. The minimum age for a man to enlist as a legionnaire was eighteen, and they must be of Roman birth. Slaves were strictly prohibited from joining the ranks; if one were caught trying to sneak their way in, they would be slain mercilessly. Initially, only those with a height of over five foot ten were allowed to sign up, but as the empire grew more desperate for soldiers—probably due to the constant warfare and terrible plagues that had robbed many lives—the height requirement was lowered to five foot eight. Soldiers were also expected to have great strength and the ability to march at least twenty miles a day while carrying multiple weapons, tent equipment, cooking pots, and other essential items on their backs. The potential recruits were put to the test, as they had to showcase their battle prowess along with their athletic and medical skills. Once all the requirements were checked and the tests passed, they were allowed to swear an oath to the emperor and head to the barracks.

The legionnaires were not only exposed to risks and dangers during a raging war but also during their daily training. They were no strangers to cruel punishments, especially those who portrayed cowardice or were deemed incompetent by their strict commanders. During a march, centurions or commanders would keep a close eye on their soldiers while holding a vine staff in one of their hands. One small mistake, and the soldier would receive a terrible beating. One man known as Lucilius was recorded by the ancient historian Tacitus as one of the most brutal centurions in Roman history; he was believed to have beaten his legionnaires until his staff broke in two. The beating did not stop there, as he then yelled for a new staff so that he could continue the punishment. His excessive brutality proved too much for the soldiers, and he was targeted and murdered by his comrades.

Severe beatings were not the only punishments soldiers had to endure. They could also face execution if they made a serious mistake. Many commanders, even Augustus himself, used decimation, an infamous form of punishment. During decimation, the soldiers would be put into groups of ten and forced to draw lots. The unfortunate man who drew the shortest straw would be the one to get executed, often by the remaining nine soldiers in the group who bludgeoned him to death.

When it was finally time to leave the barracks and prepare for a vicious confrontation, the imperial army would ensure they were armed to the teeth. For protection, a legionnaire would wear iron armor over his simple wool tunic, along with a metal helmet, which was usually made out of either iron or bronze, depending on one's rank and wealth. A *scutum* shield, which often hung on a legionnaire's back, might have been the heaviest item they had to carry. However, the shield's versatility made it extremely useful in battle. Initially, the shield was crafted in a circular shape, but it eventually evolved into a large rectangle that covered the entire torso. While in conflict, the shield would be held in the soldier's left hand and used to parry close combat blows or to protect the body from a rain of arrows. The *scutum* also featured an iron knob at its center, which could be used to bash and stagger an enemy.

The Roman shield, *scutum*.
No machine-readable author provided. MatthiasKabel assumed (based on copyright claims)., CC BY-SA 3.0 <http://creativecommons.org/licenses/by-sa/3.0/>, via Wikimedia Commons: https://commons.wikimedia.org/wiki/File:Scutum_1.jpg

The Roman *gladius*.
CC BY-SA 3.0 <http://creativecommons.org/licenses/by-sa/3.0/>, via Wikimedia Commons: https://commons.wikimedia.org/wiki/File:Roman_gladius-transparent.png

    Legionnaires seldom carried ranged weapons, as those weapons were mostly reserved for the auxiliaries or non-citizen troops, whose main role was to assist the imperial army. Along with a *scutum*, legionnaires carried a javelin called a *pilum*. At the start of a battle, the soldiers would hurl the javelin toward their charging opponents. Some would aim at the enemies' shields to limit their defense, while others would aim for the torso. It was extremely difficult for the enemy to remove the javelin from t either their shields or body armor, thus limiting their mobility. The *pilum* was carefully designed to bend once it hit the target to prevent the enemies from reusing them. Once the enemies were overwhelmed by the javelins, the legionnaires would unsheathe their *gladius*, a type of sword, and charge toward them. With their *scutum* held tightly in their left hand, shielding them from any ranged attacks, the Roman soldiers would thrust their *gladius* into the abdomen of their enemies—a fatal spot—followed by a few short slashes. If they were too close to the enemy and had little space to maneuver, the legionnaires would switch to their secondary weapon called *pugio*, an efficient dagger used to perform quick stabs.

    The Roman army always preferred facing their enemies on the battlefield head-on, but in certain cases, they were left with no choice but to form a completely different strategy. If their enemies decided to choose defense and remain within their heavily fortified walls, the Romans' clever art of siege warfare was applied. Formidable siege towers were often used to besiege enemy settlements. To topple fortified towers surrounding a city, the army used a catapult called an onager, which could launch circular boulders weighing up to 80 kilograms (176 pounds). Other siege weapons, such as *carroballista* and *scorpions*, were used because of their high accuracy. Instead of rocks and boulders, these two ballistas fired hard iron bolts that could easily pierce armor. To break open the city walls and splinter wooden gates, battering rams were used, which were made out of long, heavy timber and a pointy metal front.

Battle Tactics and Formations

The Romans were believed to have borrowed various influences from the Greeks, including war techniques. Initially, the Roman troops were comprised of hoplites armed with a spear and shield. During a battle, they formed a type of formation known as the phalanx, which was effective, especially against cavalries. Standing less than fifty centimeters (twenty inches) apart, the hoplites interlocked their shields to provide protection and attacked enemies close by with their long spears.

However, despite the phalanx's great effectiveness and mobility, this battle formation had a major flaw; the flanks of the phalanx were often left exposed. By the 3rd century BCE, a new tactical unit was introduced, along with different formations. The military unit was known as maniple. Under a manipular legion, the army was divided into three main units: *hastati*, which comprised of heavy infantry carrying a sword and *scutum*; *principes*, which were more experienced soldiers who were typically in their late twenties; and *triarii*, the most experienced soldiers who often had enough wealth to afford the best armor and weapons. These units were also supported by cavalry units called *equites* and *velites*, the latter of which were young and less skilled soldiers who were normally placed in the front lines. At the start of a battle, the *velites* would throw their javelins toward the oncoming enemies before retreating to the back, giving way for the more experienced soldiers to advance.

By the late 2nd century BCE, the Roman military welcomed a new change in their classes and formations. The Marian reforms replaced the maniple system and entirely removed the military classes, resulting in the soldiers becoming equally trained and equipped. These heavy infantrymen were then divided into cohorts, a unit in a Roman legion. A full-strength Roman legion had about 4,800 to 5,000 well-equipped soldiers. There were ten cohorts within a legion, and each of these cohorts was split into six centuries of eighty men. Centuries were led by centurions, military commanders appointed either by the emperor or the Senate, although their comrades could also elect them. The Marian reforms also changed the way the military obtained its supplies. Soldiers were no longer expected to supply their own weapons and armor, as the reforms placed the responsibility of providing supplies on the shoulders of the military generals.

Some of the most famous battle formations used by the Roman legions were the hollow square and testudo. The hollow square, sometimes called the infantry square, was often used against cavalry. The Romans would arrange themselves closely next to each other, forming a square or, sometimes, a rectangle. This particular formation took time to form; however, once the soldiers were in position, it meant certain death for cavalrymen who dared to charge directly at them. The hollow square was famously used against the Parthian cavalry at the Battle of Carrhae. Unfortunately, the Parthians were a step ahead of the Romans, as their continued use of arrows greatly impacted the formation, breaking the Romans' defense.

The Roman army forming the testudo formation.
Cassius Ahenobarbus, CC BY-SA 3.0 <https://creativecommons.org/licenses/by-sa/3.0>, via Wikimedia Commons: https://commons.wikimedia.org/wiki/File:Colonne_trajane_1-57_(cropped).jpg

Testudo, on the other hand, was often used during a siege. The Romans, along with their heavy *scutum*, would align to form a packed formation resembling the shell of a tortoise. Testudo helped the Roman troops protect themselves from attacks coming from above, behind, and in front of them. Those at the front of the formation would hold their shields up to their eye level, while those in the back held their shields over their heads to defend themselves from any arrows or spears. However, the troops moved slowly while in this formation, as they had to move in unison. Nevertheless, testudo was used by many commanders, one of them being Mark Antony, who, according to Cassius Dio, commanded his troops into a perfect testudo formation. It was reportedly so strong that even a horse could be ridden over it.

Military Awards and Honorary Gifts

Apart from stable and attractive pay, the Roman military enjoyed several awards and gifts from the emperor. While these awards were given to honor their sacrifice and bravery, they were also used to maintain morale and loyalty. The *hasta pura*, for instance, was a type of military decoration awarded to distinguished soldiers who had proven their skill during their first campaign. Shaped to resemble a spear—though it was non-lethal due to the lack of iron in its production—the *hasta pura* was normally awarded to the chosen soldier during a victory triumph and in front of a crowd. According to Suetonius, Emperor Claudius once presented this award to his most loyal supporter and highest-ranking magistrate in Rome, Tiberius Claudius Balbilus, after he emerged victorious from a mission in Britain.

A pair of Roman *armillae* in the shape of snakes.
Walters Art Museum, Public domain, via Wikimedia Commons:
https://commons.wikimedia.org/wiki/File:Roman_-_Pair_of_Snake_Bracelets_-_Walters_57528,_57529_-_Group_(cropped).jpg

Another type of military award popular during ancient Rome was an *armilla*. This award was strictly reserved for Roman soldiers below the rank of centurion; non-citizen soldiers were not eligible for this honorary award. Recipients would receive a type of bracelet made from bronze, silver, or gold, depending on their rank and social status. These bracelets were only worn by awarded soldiers during victory triumphs or any official ceremony taking place in the Eternal City. The tradition of gifting the soldiers with bracelets first began in the mid-3rd century BCE when the Romans were at war with the Celts. The elite Celtic warriors often trampled the battlefield while wearing golden necklaces and armbands, symbols of authority and prestige. So, when the Gallic chieftain was finally defeated, Roman General Titus Manlius Torquatus took the chieftain's torque and wore it around his own neck. From there on, torques were often gifted to Roman soldiers as awards, with the addition of bracelets in the empire's later years.

During an official ceremony, some Roman soldiers could be seen with one or more circular insignia fastened on their armor. Known as phalera, which was synonymous with award medals, they often carried the images of the ruling emperor or the Roman deities, especially Jupiter and Mars. Like most Roman military awards, a phalera came in bronze, silver, and gold and could be awarded to individual soldiers or the entire unit. If it were bestowed upon a unit, the medal would be attached to their banners. At times, centurions would wear these medals on their armor to inspire their troops.

A set of phalera.
Hartmann Linge, CC BY-SA 3.0 <https://creativecommons.org/licenses/by-sa/3.0>, via Wikimedia Commons: https://commons.wikimedia.org/wiki/File:Lauersforter_Phalerae_Museum_Burg_Linn.jpg

Crowns and wreaths were also given as awards to the Roman military. The rarest award was the Grass Crown, which was only awarded to generals and commanders who had saved their legions from certain death on the battlefield. Presented by the army that he had saved, a Grass Crown, just as its name suggests, was made out of grass or plants taken from the battlefield. The Camp Crown was given to the first soldier who managed to penetrate the enemy's base or camp during a raging battle. Sometimes known as the Vallary Crown, as part of this award, the soldier would receive a golden crown in the unique shape of a palisade (high fences made out of stakes).

Those who saved the lives of Roman citizens, typically when a city was besieged, were eligible for the Civic Crown. However, the saved citizens had to confirm the soldier's bravery. Almost like the Grass Crown, the Civic Crown was not made of gold but rather oak leaves, which were then woven into a wreath. The Civic Crown was the second-highest honorary award in ancient Rome. The Roman author and naval commander of the early empire Pliny the Elder claimed that when a person with a Civic Crown on his head came to the Roman games, everyone, including the Senate, had to rise from their seats as a sign of respect.

Chapter 9 – Social Structure and Status

Many years had passed since the success of Augustus Caesar transformed the Roman Republic into a powerful empire. Although the empire was plunged into chaos after the passing of its first emperor, Rome was brought to its ultimate glory during the reign of the Five Good Emperors. A great number of military victories were achieved, many structures in Rome were successfully restored, and the empire's defense was greatly upgraded. Around this time, imperial Rome was considered one of the wealthiest and most powerful empires to exist. However, despite the empire's flourishing condition, not everyone had the opportunity to live their life peacefully.

Even before the reign of Augustus, Roman law considered those who were born in Italy as Roman citizens or *cives Romani*. Those who were born outside of Italy were referred to as *peregrini*. Although *peregrini* mostly inhabited the empire in the 1st and 2nd centuries CE, they were not considered citizens and did not have the same rights as Roman citizens. In criminal law, for instance, a *peregrinus* who had become entangled in any kind of serious crime could be tortured during official interrogations, while Roman citizens were exempted from such poor treatment. In fact, the citizens could even insist on a trial and choose to appeal his criminal sentence, be it jail time or a death sentence.

Peregrini were also subjected to an annual poll tax, *tributum capitis*, while Roman citizens were exempted from it. Since joining the military was one of the few ways to obtain wealth—should one survive the twenty-five-year-long service term—many would join the ranks without hesitation. While citizens could sign up and train as a legionnaire, a *peregrinus* was restricted from doing so. They were only allowed to enlist as auxiliaries, which offered little pay compared to the legionnaires. However, they and their children could be granted citizenship should they survive the service term.

In 212, Roman Emperor Caracalla passed the *Constitutio Antoniniana*, an edict that granted citizenship to every free man and woman in the empire. They no longer had to face different treatment than the Roman citizens. However, they were quick to realize that life as a Roman citizen was not always rainbows and sunshine, as the empire's social structure was strictly based on four main aspects: heredity, freedom, property, and wealth.

Just like many other empires and kingdoms of the ancient world, the social structure of imperial Rome was based on a hierarchical system. At the top of the hierarchy was none other than the emperor. As the person at the very top of the social pyramid, he had the ultimate authority over every matter in the empire and led a lavish life. During times of peace, they remained in the finest dwelling on Palatine Hill. Augustus established his own palace on this very hill, followed by Tiberius, who oversaw some huge expansion projects. It was only in 81 CE, during the rule of Emperor Domitian, that Palatine Hill became enclosed, separating the imperial palace from the rest of the citizens.

An emperor's wealth was poured into not only the construction of palaces, temples, and statues but also lavish banquets and parties. While sources claim that certain emperors, such as Augustus, Aurelius, Hadrian, and Trajan, never promoted excessive dinners and preferred to stick to modest banquets, other rulers never hesitated to indulge themselves with only the best foods and wines. Marcus Gavius Apicius, a Roman epicure, was believed to have served honey-glazed nightingales stuffed with prunes to Tiberius's sons.

Roman emperors often donned a solid purple toga to distinguish themselves from their subordinates and subjects—a tradition started by Julius Caesar. He may have gotten the idea from the ancient Etruscan kings. The Roman emperor's abundance of wealth and power came with a price; their position on top of the social structure was almost never perfectly secure, and assassinations and conspiracies were almost always on the table.

Nevertheless, emperors were supported by the ruling classes: the senators and patricians. Placed at the top of the hierarchy—right below the ruling emperor—both were usually wealthy landowners and leaders of Rome's most powerful and oldest family lines. Patricians (simply translated as "fathers") were the ones who held power over Rome's political sphere, religious matters, and military leadership. They were also granted many privileges compared to the rest of the social classes. For instance, patricians were exempted from certain military duties typically done by normal citizens. Only senators and patricians could become emperors.

With such privilege and power, patricians were expected to be highly educated. Young boys would be taught by private tutors in a wide range of subjects and fields, from history to geography, literature, and poetry. Some even had the opportunity to master different languages, including Greek. Wealthy girls likely would have been educated more than their plebeian counterparts. Since most men would embrace a career in the harsh political world of Rome, young patricians were taught the art of public speaking and law. But, like the Roman emperors, the life of a patrician was not simple; they were the ones who often got wrapped up in palace intrigue.

Right below the patricians was another high-ranking social class known as the equestrians, who were responsible for ensuring the empire never stopped growing. Just as the name suggests, equestrians consisted of the Roman cavalry. Early on, one could qualify as an equestrian if they were rich enough to own a horse. However, as time passed, an equestrian had to be worth at least 400,000 sesterces.

Due to the *Lex Claudia*, a Roman law passed in 218 BCE that prohibited the senators from getting involved in commercial roles, the equestrians were often involved in trade and business.

Equestrians were also given several privileges, although they were not as extensive as the patricians and senators. Should an equestrian gain enough wealth throughout his career, he could step up to the next rank and become a senator. Those who belonged to the equestrian class were allowed to wear a tunic decorated with a clavus, a set of purple vertical stripes that ran from the top of their shoulders down to their leg. The stripes were, of course, thinner than those worn by the senators to distinguish their rank.

As their numbers increased to the point where they surpassed the senators, Augustus began to take notice of their importance. He reorganized the equestrians into a military class and gave them more positions in the government. Those who portrayed great potential while serving in the army had the chance of getting promoted to prefect, government administrator, or even procurator or imperial governor.

Moving down the hierarchy, we find the plebeians, which comprised the majority of Roman citizens. These working individuals, which included farmers, craftsmen, artisans, bakers, and blacksmiths, were neither rich nor poor. Historians suggest that most plebeians were illiterate compared to the elites, who had easy access to education. Most of the plebeians lived their lives with the simple aim of earning enough money to pay taxes and support their families. Those ambitious enough to rise through the social pyramid worked hard to save money and take their place among the equestrians. Despite having no power in politics and official government matters, plebeians could become a threat to the elites whenever there were cases of injustice. Even Augustus was well aware of the danger the plebeians posed; hence, he always ensured the commoners were well-fed and reasonably entertained.

At the bottom of the Roman social structure were the slaves. The Romans obtained their slaves in various ways. Since Roman slavery was not based on race, prisoners of war, captured enemies, and unfortunate individuals sold by pirates were the most common sources of slaves. There were also plenty of cases where poor parents were forced to sell their children into slavery so that they could live to see another day.

A depiction of a slave market in ancient Rome.
https://commons.wikimedia.org/wiki/File:Jean-L%C3%A9on_G%C3%A9r%C3%B4me_004.jpg

Like all forms of slavery around the globe, slaves had no personal rights, and their days were filled with nothing but hurdles and obstacles. Once they had been bought, they became the property of their owners. One small mistake, and they could face several different harsh punishments. Beatings were not unusual, and all of the slaves were familiar with the cruel insults thrown into their faces every single day. Their owners could also kill them at any moment without worrying about being persecuted by the Roman court of law.

Roman mosaic depicting two slaves in their typical clothing carrying wine.
Pascal Radigue, CC BY 3.0 <https://creativecommons.org/licenses/by/3.0>, via Wikimedia Commons: https://commons.wikimedia.org/wiki/File:Mosaique_echansons_Bardo.jpg

Work never ended for the slaves, and their owners could send them to various places. Some worked in private households, where their main responsibilities were to take care of their owner's children, while some were sent to mines, factories, or farms. Many also worked to complete all kinds of construction projects across the empire; they built long stretches of roads for the military, as well as pavements, aqueducts, sewer systems, statues, and other structures. A great number of them—usually those who had been prisoners of war—were forced to fight to their death in gladiatorial games.

However, the slaves could obtain freedom. Those lucky enough to have been bought by kind-hearted owners were sometimes freed after several years of loyal service. Those who were less fortunate had to resort to manumission. Once slaves earned enough savings, they could buy their freedom. Freed slaves were granted citizenship and allowed to work the same jobs as plebeians. The father of the famous Roman poet Horace was believed to have been a freedman who had successfully bought his freedom after being enslaved for several long years. Freedmen and Freedwomen gained personal rights and were only prohibited from holding official positions in the government. However, a different law applied to children born to freemen; they were allowed to rise through the ranks and hold office.

The Roles of Women in the Roman Empire

Historians believed that women in ancient Egypt generally had the same rights and standards as men; not only were they allowed to have their own businesses, but female rulers were also common in Egypt. Greeks, on the other hand, had different views. Women in ancient Greece rarely enjoyed privileges and were confined to the home. But what about the roles of women in the Roman Empire? Did they get to live on the same level as the men, or did they have to endure different treatment and perhaps injustice?

It is safe to assume that the two genders were, of course, treated differently. Marriage was one of the most important aspects of a Roman woman's life. It was common for girls to be married off to the man of her father's choosing at a young age—some were expected to tie the knot as soon as they reached puberty, but most were married at the age of twenty. Once a woman had a family of her own, her main responsibility was tending to the household and taking care of the children. But this was not always the case with women of higher classes. The elites would often leave their children under the care of servants or hired caregivers. With their children off of their hands during the day, elite women would spend their time studying either philosophy or literature. Women of all classes were allowed to go to the theater, public baths, races, and gladiatorial games. Some women even chose to become gladiators and competed in the arena.

In the eyes of the Romans, women were seen as fully dependent on their husbands or the male leader of their families. Cicero viewed women as having weak judgment compared to men. He suggested placing restrictions on them when it came to managing their property. But much to his disappointment, the suggestion was not legalized. Although some men agreed with Cicero's point of view, Roman law stated that parents were allowed to distribute properties among their sons and daughters evenly. This explains why one could sometimes find women who actually had their own estates and businesses.

The Roman political world was fully reserved for men. Regardless of social stature, women were not allowed to cast their votes or voice their opinions in political assemblies. However, some women were clever enough to assert their influence indirectly. Mothers would voice their interests regarding a certain political matter through their sons. This can be seen during the reigns of a few emperors. For instance, it is said Tiberius's mother controlled his decisions until he finally removed her from his life. Some believe that the barrack emperor Severus Alexander was heavily influenced by his mother's ideas, eventually leading to their demise.

Early 18th-century depiction of the dedication of a Vestal Virgin.
https://commons.wikimedia.org/wiki/File:Alessandro_Marchesini_-_Dedication_of_a_New_Vestal_Virgin_-_WGA14054.jpg

Perhaps the most esteemed position a woman in the empire could hold was the priestess of Vesta, known as the Vestal Virgin. However, the role was not voluntary; they had to be chosen from a highborn family. Once a girl was chosen (they were handpicked at the age of six to twelve) by the chief priest, the priestess had to remain chaste for at least thirty years. To ensure they could dedicate themselves entirely to Vesta, the goddess of the hearth, the priestess would be removed from her family and made legally independent. She also had to move out of her family home to the House of the Vestal Virgins, which was next to the sacred temple. After thirty years of serving the goddess with their chastity, these women would end up with enough wealth to last for the rest of their lives. Although they were free to marry once they were freed from the priesthood, many chose to remain independent.

Chapter 10 – Arts and Architecture

Military campaigns, warfare, and assassinations might have been familiar to the ancient Roman world. But aside from the continuous skirmishes and conspiracies, the Romans were well known for their exquisite architecture and complex engineering. Take the Roman aqueducts for example. Historians believe the Romans began building aqueduct systems as early as 312 BCE. Using gravity and natural slopes, the aqueducts typically transported fresh water from natural lakes or springs. The Romans used the clean water for various purposes: drinking, farming, mining, and supplying the many public baths, fountains, and even latrines scattered throughout the highly populated Roman cities.

The Roman emperors often commissioned these stone-arched aqueducts to improve the lives of the citizens. Each structure had its own specific design, source area, and water quality. Archaeologists claim that by the 3rd century CE, the city of Rome alone had eleven aqueducts in total, supplying clean water to over ninety kilometers away. Some of these ancient aqueducts survived for us to marvel at today, such as the Aqua Virgo, which was built during the reign of Augustus and is currently used to supply the world-famous Trevi Fountain.

The Roman Forum

The Eternal City was believed to have embraced seven different hills within its ancient walls. Two of the most popular ones were Capitoline Hill and Palatine Hill. While the latter went down in history as the "Nucleus of the Roman Empire," Capitoline Hill was regarded as Rome's most sacred site. On top of the enchanted hill, which was also known as Mons Saturnius, was the Temple of Jupiter. Although the temple is forever lost to history, it was once considered the most important Roman temple. Constructed in 509 BCE to honor Jupiter—the Roman equivalent of Zeus—the temple faced many destructive episodes. It was continuously restored and rebuilt by the Roman emperors until a terrible attack by the Vandals in the mid-5th century CE permanently destroyed it.

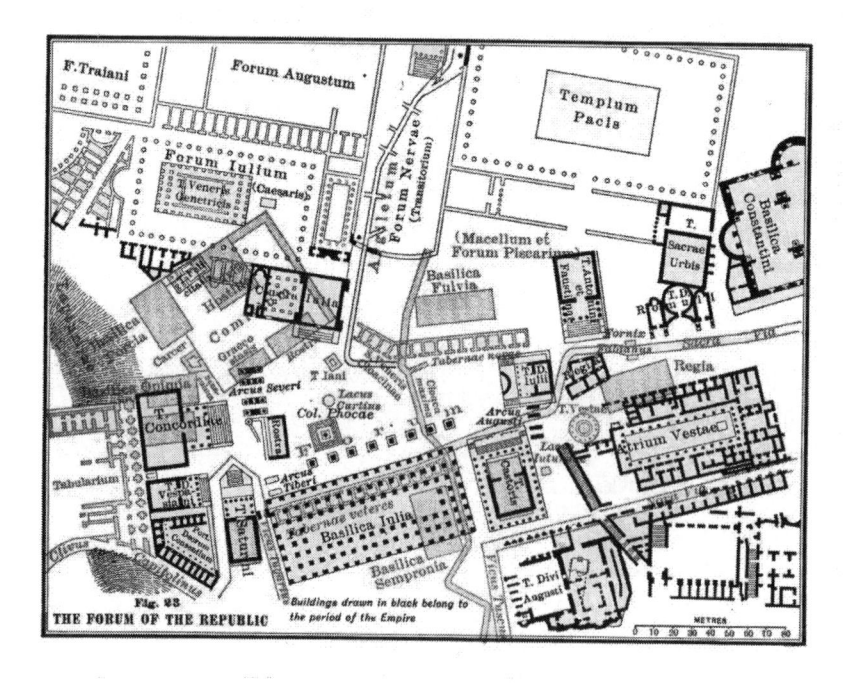

Map of the Roman Forum.
https://commons.wikimedia.org/wiki/File:Platner-forum-republic-96_recontructed_color.jpg

About 40 meters (131 feet) below the two hills was the Roman Forum. Since a huge lake occupied the majority of the site, the Romans had no choice but to drain the water before they could start building anything. Using an underground sewer system called

Cloaca Maxima, the water was successfully diverted to a nearby river. Initially, the area was developed as a marketplace, but as time went by, several massive construction projects began to take place, converting the valley into the center of the Eternal City.

Back in those days, the Roman Forum almost never slept; it was constantly filled with Roman citizens conducting both formal business and religious matters. The Basilica Julia, built to commemorate Julius Caesar, was one of the most prominent structures in the Forum. It was mainly used as a court of justice, but when Christianity was made the empire's official religion, the basilica acted as an important church. The Temple of Vesta, which housed the sacred fire of the hearth goddess, Vesta, could also be found at the Forum.

Remains of the ancient Roman Forum.
BeBo86, CC BY-SA 3.0 <https://creativecommons.org/licenses/by-sa/3.0>, via Wikimedia Commons: https://commons.wikimedia.org/wiki/File:Forum_romanum_6k_(5760x2097).jpg

Aside from temples, columns, and statues of emperors, the Romans were also known for their triumphal arches. While the oldest triumphal arch is the Arch of Augustus, the Triumphal Arch of Septimius Severus is perhaps the most intricate and complex. Still standing today, despite being heavily damaged, the triple triumphal arch was erected to commemorate the Romans' victory over Parthia in the 2nd century CE. Certain scenes of the successful military campaign were depicted on the relief panels, along with ornate columns and sculptures of ancient gods, especially Mars, occupying the rest of the arch.

The Colosseum, the Roman Empire's Largest Amphitheater

The Roman Colosseum is a notable structure, not only during the ancient period but also in modern times. Today, the partly destroyed amphitheater remains a sight to behold, but back then, this spectacular structure was built not only to impress but also to hold bloody and vicious events: the gladiatorial games.

The plan to construct the enormous amphitheater was first laid out sometime around 70 CE. However, Emperor Vespasian did not get to see the completed structure since he died several years later. The project was carried on by Emperor Titus, and in 80 CE, the Colosseum was finally opened to the public. Known as the Flavian Amphitheatre back then, Titus announced a hundred days of games when the amphitheater opened. Gladiatorial and wild animal fights were some of the games held, keeping the Roman citizens greatly entertained.

The construction of such a massive stone structure required a lot of plans, complicated calculations, and, of course, labor. Its location, for instance, was chosen for a reason. The Colosseum was built to the east of the Roman Forum, right on the site of Nero's golden palace: the very same palace that he had built for himself after confiscating many Roman citizens' properties. Vespasian, who sought to reverse the damage that Nero and his successors had done a few decades back, chose the site of Nero's palace on purpose and commissioned the construction of the Colosseum as a gift to his people.

The world-famous Roman Colosseum.
FeaturedPics, CC BY-SA 4.0 <https://creativecommons.org/licenses/by-sa/4.0>, via Wikimedia Commons: https://commons.wikimedia.org/wiki/File:Colosseo_2020.jpg

The iconic amphitheater was carefully designed by professional Roman architects, engineers, and artists, but the heavy construction work was mostly done by Jewish slaves—it was believed that at least twenty thousand of them (if not more) were involved in the building of the massive structure. The main construction material, travertine stones, could only be quarried in Albulae, a location believed to be located near modern-day Tivoli. Transporting the stones was no doubt a hassle due to the distance, so new roads were built from the quarry straight to the construction site. It is said that over 200,000 carts filled with travertine stones were transported in the span of the 8-year construction period.

Aside from its size—sources claim that the full size of the Colosseum was about 190 by 155 meters (623 by 508 feet)—the most prominent features were its columns and arched entrances. The structure consisted of three stories and eighty arched entrances, which were fully supported by impressive semi-circular columns. The columns varied depending on the stories. The first story featured simple Doric columns. The second floor had Ionic columns, while the third story featured a set of ornate Corinthian columns. Inside, the Colosseum could fit up to fifty thousand spectators. However, it is plausible that seating was arranged according to social class.

The amphitheater was used for nearly four centuries. Later on, as gladiatorial fights and other forms of ancient entertainment were put to a stop—especially when the Western Roman Empire was about to collapse—the structure was abandoned, and its materials were quarried for new construction projects. Due to a series of natural disasters that struck the empire and the erosion of time, only a third of the Colosseum has survived today.

Roman Baths

As part of providing entertainment for the people, the Roman emperors commissioned the construction of public baths. Historians suggest this idea originated when the Romans visited the towns of the ancient Greeks. The Romans were well known for assimilating the architectural styles of the Greeks, so it is not surprising that they decided to create a public bath in each Roman town across the empire. Typically built near the forum of Roman cities, the Romans expanded the concept of these public baths to include several other facilities. While the Greeks only had hip-baths, the Romans included a set of changing rooms called the *apodyterium*, an exercise room or gymnasium, an open-air swimming pool referred to as *natatio*, massage rooms, and much else. Fountains, gardens, libraries, and lecture halls were also among the features of a Roman public bath.

These baths were often swarmed by the Romans, especially around noon to dusk. Everyone was allowed to spend time at the baths, no matter their social status. Slaves would normally enter if their owners chose to bring them along; they were usually tasked with carrying their owner's belongings, ranging from bathing garments to linen towels, sandals, and other equipment. While entrance to other forms of entertainment in Rome, such as the gladiatorial games, was free, Romans had to pay an entrance fee to use the public baths. However, the fee was so small that even the poorest of citizens could easily afford it. Scholars claim that by the time of Diocletian, the entrance fee for public baths was placed at only two denarii. Free entrance to the baths could be enjoyed during public holidays or any other important festivities.

Augustus's right-hand man and closest friend, Marcus Vipsanius Agrippa, was responsible for constructing Rome's first public baths or *thermae*. It was completed as early as 25 BCE, and the waters of the bath were supplied through the aqueduct Aqua Virgo, which was thought to have been built mainly for the baths. Other outstanding examples of Roman baths were the Lepcis Magna, the Baths of Diocletian in the heart of Rome, the Antonine Baths, and the Baths of Caracalla in southern Rome. The latter is considered by historians and archeological experts alike as the best-preserved Roman baths to ever survive.

Built sometime around the 3rd century CE, the Baths of Caracalla were regarded as the most luxurious Roman baths to ever exist, not only in the ancient period but also by modern standards. The entire complex was said to have been built with nearly 7 million bricks and consisted of over 250 interior columns. The size of the complex was so massive that it could cater to up to eight thousand visitors a day. Two sumptuous libraries, a watermill, a gymnasium, an Olympic-size swimming pool, six-foot long fountains, and a waterfall were some of the Baths of Caracalla's most prominent features.

An illustration of the once glorious Baths of Caracalla.
Lruiz094, CC BY-SA 4.0 <https://creativecommons.org/licenses/by-sa/4.0>, via Wikimedia Commons:
https://commons.wikimedia.org/wiki/File:%22Reconstruction_drawing_of_the_Baths_of_Caracalla,_Caelian_Hill,_Rome%22_.jpg

Back in the baths' heyday, one could look around and find exquisite marble and granite adorning every inch of the walls. Parts of the ceiling were made out of finely crafted glass mosaic, which created unique iridescent patterns of the pool when light was reflected at certain angles. Separating two of the three main chambers of the baths—the *frigidarium* and the *tepidarium*—was the great hall, which showcased vaulted nave ceilings, a feature that influenced most churches during the medieval period. By the 5th century CE, the Baths of Caracalla earned its spot as one of the seven wonders of Rome. However, decades later, the baths were abandoned due to the attacks on Rome. It finally fell into disuse by the 7th century, with most parts of the complex destroyed when an earthquake struck the city in 847.

Roman Art and Sculptures

Aside from figure painting, sculptures were regarded as the highest form of art in the eyes of the imperial Romans. Just like many of the empire's architectural styles, it is safe to assume that Greek art had a powerful influence on the Romans, as many of the empire's paintings and sculptures sported obvious features that were only visible in ancient Greece. The Romans were known to have a fondness for Greek-style sculptures and commissioned many marble versions of popular Greek works, such as the *Doryphoros*. The original *Doryphoros* was believed to have been made out of bronze, but it was lost sometime in the 5th century BCE. Thanks to the Romans, a few marble copies of this well-known Greek sculpture were preserved, allowing us to get an idea of what the original looked like.

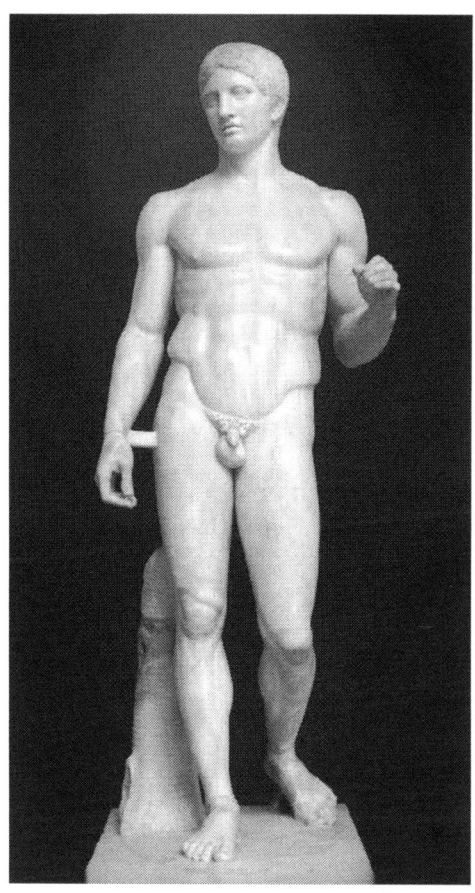

A well-preserved Roman period copy of the *Doryphoros*.
Naples National Archaeological Museum, CC BY 2.5
<*https://creativecommons.org/licenses/by/2.5*>, via Wikimedia Commons:
https://commons.wikimedia.org/wiki/File:Doryphoros_MAN_Napoli_Inv6011-2.jpg

Even historians agree that Augustus and the rest of the emperors from the Julio-Claudian dynasty were fond of classical Greek art. The best example of Roman sculpture could be the *Augustus of Primaporta*, which was commissioned at the end of the emperor's long life. Although Augustus was seventy-five when he died, the fine sculpture depicts a younger version of him, back when he first brought the empire to its utmost glory.

Emperor Hadrian, a lover of all things Greek, collected copies of the most famous Greek mosaic paintings at his villa. The *Battle of the Centaurs and Wild Beasts* by the Greek painter Zeuxis was one of his many prized possessions.

Augustus of Primaporta with a depiction of Cupid by his right leg.
https://commons.wikimedia.org/wiki/File:Statue-Augustus.jpg

    As the years passed, Roman art moved away from the classical Greek-inspired style and welcomed the art of late antiquity. Unlike the realistic sculptures of the classical period, the arts produced during this era were stiff and less realistic. This can be seen in the relief panels on the late Roman Empire's triumphal arches, such as the Arch of Septimius Severus or the Arch of Constantine in Rome. This form of art usually featured deep, full lines with the most important figure a larger size compared to the others. Despite its differences from the previous art style and the lack of naturalism, this form of art continued to be widely used during the reign of Constantine and his successors.

War relief on the Arch of Septimius Severus, a great example of the Roman art of late antiquity.

Jean-Pol GRANDMONT, CC BY 4.0 <https://creativecommons.org/licenses/by/4.0>, via Wikimedia Commons: https://commons.wikimedia.org/wiki/File:0_Arc_de_Septime_S%C3%A9v%C3%A8re_-_Rome_(5).JPG

Chapter 11 – Daily Life and Customs

It was a day almost like any other; a fellow Roman, belonging to neither an aristocratic family nor the rich, had risen from a short sleep and readied himself for yet another tiring day. Dressed in his simple tunic, the man walked through the narrow streets of the ancient Roman city to the shores of the Mediterranean, where he would embark on his boat and spend the rest of the day in the middle of nowhere, surrounded by the deep sea. While fishing was not one of the Roman Empire's main activities, this man was not a typical fisherman who spent his day under the sun waiting for red mullet to take the bait. Instead, he harvested snails collected in traps he installed on floats a few days before. The snails were *Hexaplex trunculus*, commonly known as the banded-dye murex, and used to produce purple dye for the emperor's togas.

Using techniques discovered by the Phoenicians, the man would crush these spiky snails once he had collected enough—at least ten thousand of them were needed to produce a gram of dye—and leave them under the sun to oxidize. The snails were then boiled in tin vats for a few days, filling the air with an unpleasant odor. Producing this dye was time-consuming and required a lot of labor and experience, thus making it extremely valuable.

As the sky darkened, the man returned to the shore and made his journey back home. The narrow street, once quiet during the day, was now filled with all kinds of noises that would keep people from sleeping at night. Unlike those with loads of wealth, the man lived in an *insula*, a high-rise apartment building three to seven stories high—sometimes even higher. Typically built to provide shelter, especially for those not rolling in wealth, the *insulae* were known for their poor construction, despite having running water and sanitation.

Tenants were charged a certain amount of money, which was either paid annually or weekly, depending on the spaces and rooms they occupied. The ground floor, which was paid for annually, was usually more spacious and had several rooms for different activities, such as dining and sleeping. Spaces on the higher floors were much more confined and did not have many windows. It is safe to assume that even during ancient times, no one would say that an *insula* was the best place to stay. One's safety was not guaranteed, and the rooms were usually too hot during the summer and too cold when winter arrived.

Nevertheless, the *insulae* were mostly found in Rome, the heart of the empire itself. By 150 BCE, the city already had over forty-six thousand *insulae* built for its citizens. This was due to the limited space and land in Rome, making it difficult for the city to house the increasing population; the empire had already reached at least forty-five million (some scholars believe sixty million) by the reign of Augustus. However, with brick, timber, and later Roman concrete as the *insulae's* main construction materials, they were susceptible to fire and cave-ins. Given the dark, narrow, and broken roads that led to these apartments, any sort of aid or emergency help wouldn't have been able to reach the people in time if any catastrophic situations happened. These roads were reconstructed and widened under Emperor Nero's reign after the events of the Great Fire of Rome, which burned two-thirds of the city.

Surviving *insulae* in the Roman harbor city of Ostia.
iessi, CC BY 2.0 <https://creativecommons.org/licenses/by/2.0>, *via Wikimedia Commons:* https://commons.wikimedia.org/wiki/File:Ostia_Antica-strada01-modified.jpg

While the commoners spent their lives in the easily destroyed and crowded *insulae*, the rich made themselves comfortable in a type of townhouse called a *domus*. Unlike the *insulae*, which housed several families on multiple stories, the Roman *domus* was inhabited by only a single family. The size of a *domus* varied: some people lived in a very small yet safe and comfortable house, while others lived in huge, luxurious mansions. However, what they had in common was their location: they were built close to buildings of importance and faced away from the busy streets to ensure both safety and privacy.

The atrium of a Roman *domus*.
https://commons.wikimedia.org/wiki/File:Atrium_interior.jpg

In contrast to the dilapidated *insulae*, which were rather confined and lacked natural lighting, the *domus* featured at least five different spaces and rooms, each with beautifully painted walls. Indoor courtyards, gardens, bedrooms, a dining room, private bathrooms, and a kitchen were the most common spaces in a *domus*, although some featured an office with its very own library. The most important part of this luxurious house was the atrium, which housed either an altar or a statue of a god worshiped by the household. While the rest of the atrium was usually covered by high-ceilinged porticoes, the center was left open to allow rainwater into the *impluvium*, a pool or basin designed to catch water. It was located beneath the roof opening.

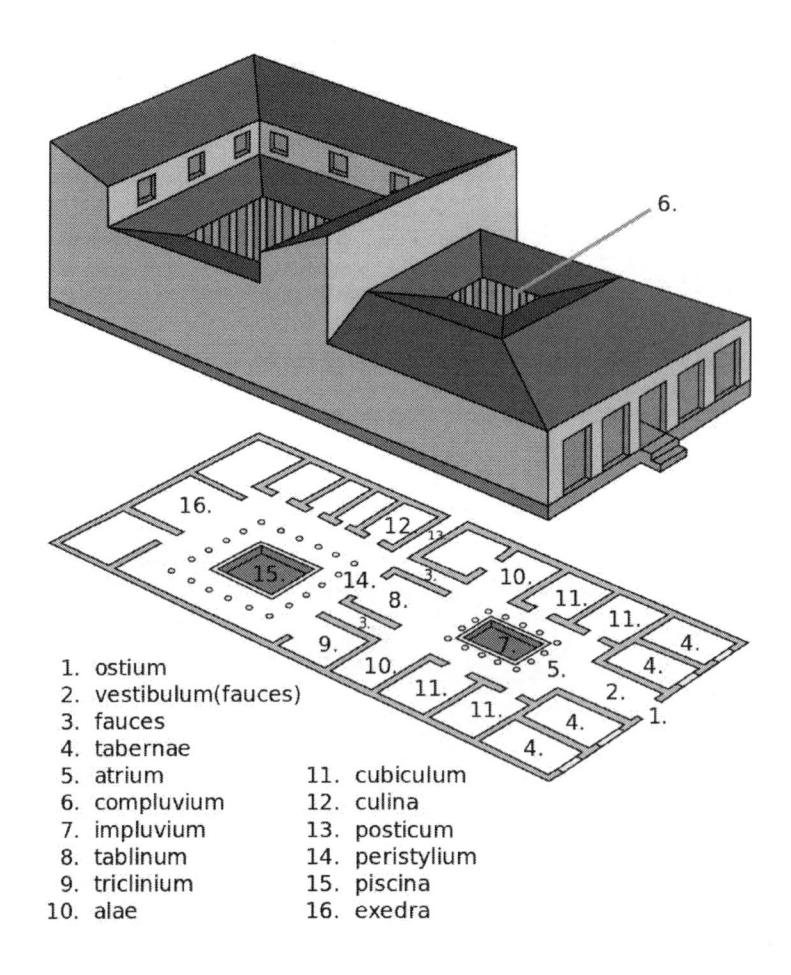

1. ostium
2. vestibulum(fauces)
3. fauces
4. tabernae
5. atrium
6. compluvium
7. impluvium
8. tablinum
9. triclinium
10. alae
11. cubiculum
12. culina
13. posticum
14. peristylium
15. piscina
16. exedra

A schematic of a *domus*.

Domus_romana_Vector001.svg: *PureCorederivative work: PureCore (talk)derivative work: Papa Lima Whiskey 2, CC BY-SA 3.0 <http://creativecommons.org/licenses/by-sa/3.0/>, via Wikimedia Commons: https://commons.wikimedia.org/wiki/File:Domus_romana_Vector002.svg

Weddings, Family Customs, and Tradition

Most marriages in ancient Rome did not start with a romantic relationship. Instead, they were arranged between two families. Parents with a son who had just stepped into his early twenties would seek a woman of their choice, although she would normally be a teenager. Once they found the perfect match, the couple had to meet a few requirements set by the law before proceeding with the wedding ceremony.

In the early years of the Roman Republic, it was strictly prohibited for freed slaves to tie the knot with any Roman citizens, but the first Roman emperor, Augustus, lifted the restriction. One of his reforms, *Lex Julia*, allowed freed slaves to marry anyone except senators. Citizens were also forbidden from marrying their close relatives, prostitutes, and actors (these two professions belonged to the lowest class). As long as these rules were met, a couple would be granted permission called *conubium*, which allowed them to continue with the wedding.

Wedding ceremonies could take place anytime throughout the year, but most Romans chose to get married in June in conjunction with Juno, the goddess of marriage (June is named after her). When the day of the wedding ceremony finally came, the groom would lead a procession to the bride's family house, which was followed by an exchange of gifts and the bride's dowry. The bride and groom signed a written document containing each other's agreement and then sealed it with a kiss. The joyous ceremony would continue with a generous feast and another procession of the newlyweds to their new home.

The process of divorce was rather simple in comparison. A couple who no longer saw eye to eye only had to declare their divorce, although some sources suggest they had to do so in the company of seven witnesses. Once divorced, the dowry had to be returned to the ex-wife so that she could begin a new life or remarry. Children were put under the custody of their father.

Ancient Rome was undoubtedly a man's world; men were on top of every matter across the empire, whether it came to politics or family matters. In a Roman household, the husband or the family's leader was referred to as the *paterfamilias*, meaning "father of the family." To put it in simple words, *paterfamilias* held absolute power in their household and could decide on a matter without question. A father could disown his child no matter the reason. Cold-hearted ones would kill their children if they did not sit right with them, while those who were not so brutal would sell their offspring as slaves. This not only applied to grown children but also newborns. Once a wife gave birth, the midwife would place the newborn on the ground. The father would approach and pick the newborn up if he wanted to accept the baby, while unwanted babies would remain on the floor.

The family's property and wealth were also owned and managed by the *paterfamilias*. They even provided a special allowance called a *peculium* to their sons. It was normal for the Romans to treat their sons differently than their daughters, as sons were considered valuable to the family line; they were expected to carry their family name should their father pass. Those families who did not have a son usually resorted to adoption.

Roman Fashion

Speaking of ancient Roman fashion, many might have imagined the Romans wearing off-white togas and a pair of sandals. However, to the surprise of many, the Romans did not always dress in the iconic toga pictured in many modern movies and TV shows. In fact, a toga was formal attire usually worn to distinguish high social statuses. There was more than one type of toga worn by the rich. *Toga virilis*, an all-white toga, was donned by wealthy young men who had just reached adulthood, while candidates for office typically wore the chalk-white *toga candida*. The *toga praetexta*, which was decorated with a purple stripe, was only allowed for senators and high priests. The rarest of all was the solid purple and golden embroidered *toga picta*, which were strictly reserved for emperors.

As for women, their formal attire was called the stola. The long, sleeveless garment could only be worn by married women. Since a stola was rather simple, women often elevated their looks with elaborate hairstyles and jewelry. Unmarried women wore only a simple tunic—similar to what lower-class men and children would have worn.

Indoors, the Romans often wore sandals—the very ones often depicted in films and paintings. However, whenever they were outdoors or on a long journey, they changed into a pair of boots typically made out of leather. These boots were available to all social classes, though the rich often opted for a more complex design. Soldiers owned a pair of more durable boots known as *caligae*.

What Did the Romans Eat?

At daybreak, it was normal for the Romans to start their day with *ientaculum* or a simple breakfast. Since it was the first meal of the day, a piece of bread from the bakery would suffice, which, most of the time, would be enjoyed with slices of cheese and watered-down wine. Those who could not afford bread would eat staple porridge made from boiled spelt, wheat, or millet. A few aromatic spices and vegetables were added to the porridge to enhance the flavor, and there was usually some fruit on the side.

At high noon, the Romans would rest and sit for a quick lunch called *prandium*, which consisted of salted bread, cheese, fruit, and possibly fish, meat, or eggs. While all Roman citizens ate chicken eggs, large goose eggs were considered luxurious and more often consumed by the rich. Dinner was the main meal of the day. Lower-class citizens typically ate dinner after sunset in taverns, inns, or market stalls. Aristocrats might eat their supper while reclining on intricate couches in a luxurious dining room.

Those of the upper class started their dinner with a *gustatio* or appetizer, indulging themselves with seafood and eggs. Moving on to the main course, they would often get served with heavier options—meats and vegetables for the commoners and more exotic items, such as sea urchins, raw oysters, boars, and sometimes even flamingos and peacocks, for the wealthy. Garum, a type of fish sauce, was commonly used in dishes to elevate the taste. When in season, apples were a favorite dessert. Grapes, dates, pomegranates, and figs paired with honey, cream, or cheese were common desserts.

What Did the Romans Do for Leisure?

The Romans were lovers of entertainment. The Forum, the center of Rome where citizens conducted their business, was often busy at the crack of dawn, but it would be quiet in the evening and sometimes right after lunch. Markets began to close their doors, the elites would disperse from their important meetings, and the farmers would put down their hoes and sickles to get ready for some entertainment. Some would spend the evening watching plays and musicals. Those who preferred a more relaxing activity would travel to the public baths. They enjoyed hot baths, socializing, swimming, reading, and exercising at the gymnasium.

A depiction of a chariot race held in the Circus Maximus.
https://commons.wikimedia.org/wiki/File:Jean_L%C3%A9on_G%C3%A9r%C3%B4me_-_Chariot_Race_-_1983.380_-_Art_Institute_of_Chicago.jpg

The most popular types of entertainment in imperial Rome were none other than chariot races and gladiatorial fights, both of which were some of the most violent sports to ever exist in history. Chariot races were held in the Circus Maximus, the largest Roman stadium or hippodrome nestled in between the two hills of Rome. This extreme sport, which could trace its roots back to the early foundation of Rome in the 8th century BCE, was believed to be intertwined with the ancient Roman religion. Because of that, the event always began with a sacred procession of the chariot drivers, who were accompanied by a big group of dancers, musicians, and several statues of Roman gods through the streets of Rome.

The race would take place on the two-thousand-foot-long sand track. The chariot racers would burst through the gates at the starting line once a white handkerchief was dropped on the ground by the game's sponsor. These daring drivers would then steer their chariots to maximum speed—some reached at least forty miles per hour—before testing their skills at the turns. Chariot crashes and injuries were a common sight, which explains why there were always attendants near the tracks ready to rush in and clear the way before another lap took place. After a total of seven laps, the chariot racer who finished first would be celebrated with the sounds of trumpets before being led to the judges' box, where they would be given their victory wreath and prize money.

Gladiatorial fights were held in the famous Colosseum. The bloody fights were held around eight to twelve times per year. They were normally sponsored by the ruling emperor to not only provide entertainment to his subjects but also avoid revolts. Other than weapon combat and wild animal fights, there were reenactments of naval battles, though this particular event was extremely rare.

During a gladiatorial fight, the entire stadium would be filled with loud chants from the fifty thousand spectators. The gladiators, most of whom were either prisoners of war, criminals condemned to death, or slaves, would enter the arena bearing weapons they had mastered—the *gladius* and mace were among the most used weapons. They would then fight, swinging and thrusting their blades into one another while the crowds cheered.

A scene depicting a gladiatorial game.
https://commons.wikimedia.org/wiki/File:Jean-Leon_Gerome_Pollice_Verso.jpg

Although death and bloodbaths were fairly common in a gladiatorial game, losing a fight did not always mean certain death. Their fates also depended on the sponsors of the games, as they were the ones who set the rules. If the sponsors were not planning to watch a fight to the death, the winning gladiator could accept their opponents' surrender. The spectators could also influence the winning gladiator's decision on whether to spare or kill their losing opponent.

While the gladiatorial games were considered one of Rome's main entertainment forms, their prominence began to deteriorate as the empire began to embrace Christianity. In 325 CE, the emperor Constantine banned the games due to humanitarian reasons; the fights were seen as the opposite of civil and domestic peace.

Chapter 12 – Religion and Education

Rome was one of the most powerful empires in the Western world. However, the empire was not the Western world's earliest civilization. In fact, Rome only sprang to life in the 8th century BCE, millennia after the birth of Greece. However, the Italian Peninsula was known to have been in contact with Greece for a very long time, which led to the assimilation of Greek culture and religion. Like the Greeks, the Romans were a polytheistic civilization, which meant they worshiped multiple gods at once.

Since they were influenced by the Greeks, the Roman pantheon mostly corresponded with the Greek Olympians. Three of Rome's most important gods were Jupiter, Juno, and Minerva, who were respectively referred to as Zeus, Hera, and Athena in the Greek pantheon. Other important deities of the ancient Roman religion included Neptune, Venus, and Mars, who corresponded to Poseidon, Aphrodite, and Ares in Greek mythology. The ancient Romans also believed these gods played a role in the founding of their city.

Mars, the god of war, was believed to have born two sons with a woman named Rhea Silvia—there are some sources that claim Hercules bore these children instead of Mars. But since Rhea Silvia had sworn a vow of celibacy, her pregnancy meant certain death. At that time, it was common for those who had broken their vows to be buried alive. However, Amulius, the king of a pre-Roman city called Alba Longa, chose to spare Rhea Silvia to avoid the wrath of Mars. Instead, the king sent her to prison while he condemned her two infant children to death by one of three methods: live burial, exposure to the elements, or death by drowning in the Tiber River. The king did not want to stain his hands, so he directed his servant to carry out the murder.

The shepherd bringing Romulus and Remus home to his wife.
https://commons.wikimedia.org/wiki/File:Mignard_-_The_Shepherd_Faustulus_Bringing_Romulus_and_Remus_to_His_Wife.jpg

Looking at the infants, whose names were Romulus and Remus, the servant couldn't help but feel pity. He decided to place them inside a basket and allowed them to float down the River Tiber. Under the care of the river god Tiberinus, the two infants survived and were found by a she-wolf who suckled them. Later on, both

Romulus and Remus were discovered and adopted by a shepherd and his wife. They grew up to become shepherds, but the two got in trouble, which led to Remus being captured and presented before King Amulius himself. With haste, Romulus went to save his brother, killing the king in the process. They were then offered the throne by the citizens; however, the brothers insisted on starting their own city.

So, they set out on a journey to find the best location for their new city. Romulus suggested building the foundation on Palatine Hill, while Remus chose Aventine Hill. This disagreement turned into a quarrel, which led to Romulus building trenches and walls surrounding Palatine Hill. To mock his brother, Remus made fun of the walls and attempted to jump over them. Most stories say that Romulus then killed his brother, which some believed to be a sign from the gods that they favored Romulus's location.

Mourning the death of his brother, Romulus buried him with full respect. On the same day of the funeral, which was, according to tradition, April 21st, 753 BCE, Romulus founded Rome, a city named after himself. As the first king of Rome, Romulus ruled the city until his death. Due to his accomplishments, Romulus was believed to have become a god—a practice that was normalized by emperors due to their claim of being descended from the gods themselves. Later on, under the Roman imperial cult, the Senate would cast votes on whether or not their deceased emperor would rise to a state of divinity.

As Rome grew into a bigger city, expanding its power over different kingdoms and eventually becoming a huge empire, the Roman religion saw an explosion of various festivities and celebrations. Sometime in mid-December, the Romans gathered around to celebrate Saturnalia, a celebration in honor of Saturn, the Roman god of agriculture. During this time of the year, all businesses, schools, and even the court of law would close their doors to prepare for a grand celebration. Out of all the religious celebrations in Rome, Saturnalia was considered the most exciting and lively. Catullus, the Roman poet, described it as the best of times. Even the Roman author Pliny had to lock himself inside a soundproof room to work due to the joyous noise of the people celebrating.

The Romans celebrating Saturnalia.
*Themadchopper, Antoine-François Callet, CC0, via Wikimedia Commons:
https://commons.wikimedia.org/wiki/File:Saturnalia_by_Antoine_Callet.jpg*

Houses in Rome would be decorated with wreaths and much greenery. The week was filled with nothing but feasts, gambling, singing, and music. A gift exchange was a common practice, with taper candles called *cerei* being the most popular gift. When the Temple of Saturn was built in the 4th century CE, another ritual was brought to life, as young pigs were sacrificed in front of the public.

Another major festival was called Cerealia. It was celebrated in honor of the grain goddess Ceres, who was especially honored by the commoners. Held around mid- to late April—possibly from the 12th to the 18th—the week-long Cerealia festival was celebrated in hopes that the goddess would bestow good harvests.

The common activities that took place during Cerealia were circus games called Ludi Ceriales, which were normally held in the Circus Maximus. According to the records made by Ovid, the famous Roman poet, during the games, women could be seen dressed in all white, running around the arena while holding lit torches. This was done to symbolize an event in Roman mythology where Ceres searched for her daughter, Proserpina, who had been taken to the underworld by Pluto. The celebration also included horse races and theatrical performances.

Other religious festivities celebrated by the Romans included Liberalia in March to commemorate Liber, the god of wine, freedom, and fertility, and Lupercalia. The latter was celebrated every February 15th, and in contrast to the lively Saturnalia, this festival was rather bloody and violent, as it aimed to ward off evil spirits and avoid infertility. Its ritual included a sacrifice of male goats and a dog, with Roman priests smearing the sacrificed animals' blood on their faces. However, after Christianity became the official religion of the Roman Empire, these ancient celebrations began to disappear, although some fused with the new religion.

The Harsh Beginning of Christianity and How the Religion Prevailed

Rome witnessed the emergence of many religions and cults and tolerated some of their beliefs and practices, but not everyone enjoyed the same treatment. Certain religions and cults were banned or even persecuted if the Romans found them unnatural or unfit. For instance, the Celtic Druids who practiced the sacrifice of humans were wiped out by the Roman military. The Romans were also against Judaism, probably due to Rome's prolonged conflict and conquest of Judea. Tiberius was said to have forbidden the religion, and Emperor Claudius even went to the extent of banishing the Jews from the Eternal City.

Another religion the Romans were strictly against was none other than Christianity. The reasons behind this vary, but the most plausible one was due to the Christians' belief in a single god. Ancient Rome had been worshiping multiple gods ever since the earliest days of its existence. It is safe to say that Roman paganism focused more on the present; there were no exact details about the afterlife and salvation. That being said, the Romans believed the main reason to worship the gods was to gain their blessings and avoid their wrath. Refusing to do so would only result in a terrible sickness or perhaps famine or a plague. If the gods were properly worshiped and honored, the Romans would be showered with wealth, health, and military success.

The Christians believed in only their god, which led the Romans to conclude that this was a way of stating that their gods were false. Christians also refused to offer sacrifices to either the Roman gods or the emperors, a decision that was seen as disloyal to the empire. The Romans feared that the Christians' refusal to participate in any sort of pagan practice would only anger their gods, thus inviting great chaos and trouble. Every time the empire was overwhelmed with a certain crisis, even as small as a raging mob in the city, the Romans tended to point their fingers at the Christians. The persecution of Christians gradually became the norm, especially in Rome.

The greatest and most infamous persecution to ever take place within the Roman Empire was done by Emperor Nero. The emperor was already unpopular among some, if not all, of his subjects. So, when a sudden fire broke out that engulfed almost two-thirds of the Eternal City, the emperor was left with no choice but to look for a scapegoat in order to shift the citizens' anger and blame. The easiest targets were the Christians, who had already been demonized by many. Nero put the blame for the fire on the Christians, which resulted in a mass execution. Emperor Decius also mercilessly persecuted many Christians in 250 CE when he discovered their refusal to make a sacrifice to the Roman gods in front of officials.

When Constantine took the mantle, Christians began to see the light at the end of the tunnel. Although the persecution of Christians had ended before Constantine's reign, they were still living in fear. That was until Constantine claimed to have seen a miraculous vision of the Christian cross in his dream the night before the Battle of the Milvian Bridge in the 4th century CE. Since he emerged victorious, Constantine called himself a devout Christian, although sources suggest that he was baptized only on his deathbed. Nevertheless, Constantine was named the first Roman emperor to accept the religion with open arms.

The baptism of Constantine:
https://commons.wikimedia.org/wiki/File:Raphael_Baptism_Constantine.jpg

The emperor went on to fund and commission the construction of churches in his new capital, Constantinople. Although paganism was still practiced by some of the Romans, coexisting with Christianity and other religions, Christians could now leave the safety of their houses and participate in Roman civic life. Through the Edict of Milan, Christianity was granted legal status for the first time in history. However, after Constantine's death, Christianity's fate was yet again hung in the balance, as some reigning emperors were still skeptical of the religion. But by this period of time, the religion was growing in popularity. Finally, under the rule of Theodosius I, Christianity was made the Roman Empire's official religion, while the old pagan religion was suppressed.

Education in Imperial Rome

Education was very important in ancient Rome. However, not everyone in the empire had the luxury of being taught at school. Although the poor and commoners received some basic education, formal education, which was mostly based on the Greek system, was typically reserved for children born to wealthy families.

Girls, on the other hand, were restricted from receiving advanced education. They were only taught how to write and read, and these lessons could only be taught at their home. Some would be taught by their own mothers, while those in the higher social classes were put under the care of hired instructors. From the Romans' point of view, girls were expected to focus more on achieving their ultimate goal in life: marriage and having children. So, a Roman girl's childhood would often be filled with lessons on how to be a good wife and mother.

However, on the bright side, girls could avoid obtaining injuries caused by teachers. Education in ancient Rome was said to have been based on fear—there was even an old Roman saying that those who were never flogged were not trained. Staying true to these sayings, instructors or teachers would often beat their students with a cane or a leather whip should they make even the tiniest mistake in class. In some cases, those who made too many mistakes in a short amount of time would be held still by two slaves while their teacher beat them multiple times with a leather whip.

There were different stages of education in imperial Rome. The first one was rather informal, as it focused more on moral education, which the children received from their parents. At this stage, children would be taught various skills needed to live a life in the city, from agriculture to military skills to civil responsibilities. They were also educated about Roman tradition and ways to respect it. Basic reading, writing, and arithmetic were normally taught by the *paterfamilias* or the male leader of the family.

While the rich continued their education with private tutors, middle-class boys were sent to *ludus litterarius*, a primary school taught by a teacher referred to as a *litterator*. Back then, there was no exact location for a primary school, as it could change from one place to another. Some studied in gymnasiums or private residences, while there were others who studied in the streets. At this stage, students would mostly focus on improving their reading, writing, and mathematics. Literature was the most common teaching material, with works from Homer and Hesiod being used. Since parchment and papyrus were rather expensive at that time, students were only allowed to write on a wax tablet. Once they showed great improvement in their writing, their instructors would provide them with papyrus to write on.

At the age of nine, the rich would go on to learn more important skills from a *grammaticus*, who would sharpen his students' speaking skills. Those who had not yet mastered Greek would take this opportunity to hone their skills in the language since elite Romans were expected to be bilingual. Most of the time, these students would spend their day listening to their *grammaticus's* lectures, or *narratio*, and practicing expressive reading of poetry.

Elite students who had proved themselves through the years would be given a chance to further their studies as an orator. This level of education was crucial for those who aspired to be lawyers and politicians. Possibly originating from Greece, this level of education was not strictly taught by a teacher; instead, it was mostly done through careful observations of their elders and mentors. At this point, orators mainly focused on learning the art of public speaking while still receiving new knowledge in geography, literature, music, philosophy, mythology, and geometry—some of which were absolutely important in order to get a chance to run for office one day.

Conclusion

The Roman Empire launched numerous campaigns and introduced various laws to its many provinces. But in the end, the once-flourishing empire crumbled when Rome was taken away from its people—an event that definitely shook the world back then. The fortified walls of Rome were finally penetrated by the headstrong barbarians. Under a new ruler, the empire was split into a series of feudal kingdoms with their own code of laws, customs, and traditions. But despite the fall of Rome, the empire still managed to leave its mark and influence. In fact, certain aspects of Roman life survived and were practiced in some of these new kingdoms.

The Eastern half of the Roman Empire survived and maintained its presence in the world for about a thousand more years after its Western counterpart's defeat. With Constantinople now acting as the "New Rome," the Romans resumed their lives. Although they considered themselves part of the Roman Empire still, most scholars refer to the Eastern Roman Empire as the Byzantine Empire.

Although the mighty Roman Empire is a thing of the past, its influence can still be felt today. It had a tremendous impact on architecture, technology, law, arts, literature, and even religion. Especially in Western cultures, one could find an array of traces left by the Romans. For instance, many Roman structures survived, and some of their construction techniques were borrowed and are still used in the modern world. The Arc de Triomphe du Carrousel in

Paris is often associated with Roman architecture; its design bears a striking resemblance to the Arch of Septimius Severus in Rome.

William Shakespeare has forever been immortalized as the greatest English writer of all time, thanks to Ovid and a few other poets born during the golden period of Roman literature. The Romans' mother tongue Latin was used as the basis for the English language. Certain months in the calendar that we've come to know today owe their name to the Romans; January, March, May, and June were all named after the ancient Roman gods, while July and August were named in honor of Julius Caesar and Augustus.

The Roman concepts of laws and justice systems were widely used as a rough outline for modern-day legal systems, especially in Europe and the United States. The Roman Empire also played a key role in spreading Christianity. Although the monotheistic religion was initially rejected by the Romans, when it was finally made the official religion, its influence began to impact almost every aspect of the Romans' lives. Christmas, the most popular holiday celebrated by Christians today, traces its origins back to the Roman Empire. Some of the festivity's traditions, including gift exchanges, feasting, singing, and lighting candles, are still widely practiced today; however, they were borrowed from Saturnalia, an ancient Roman winter celebration.

With all of the triumphs and achievements obtained by the once-booming empire, it is not a surprise that the world can still feel its presence today. The Roman Empire might have faced its end over a thousand years ago, but many agree that the Romans undoubtedly helped us lay the foundations for almost every aspect of the modern world. It might be hard for us to imagine the similarities that we bear with the Romans since their lives constantly revolved around bloody wars and conquests, but it is also impossible to deny that Rome is ingrained in our lives. Despite the many violent episodes that took place throughout the years of the Roman Empire, its legacy will continue to live on and set examples for future generations to come.

Here's another book by Enthralling History that you might like

Free limited time bonus

Stop for a moment. We have a free bonus set up for you. The problem is this: we forget 90% of everything that we read after 7 days. Crazy fact, right? Here's the solution: we've created a printable, 1-page pdf summary for this book that you're reading now. All you have to do to get your free pdf summary is to go to the following website: **https://livetolearn.lpages.co/enthrallinghistory/**

Once you do, it will be intuitive. Enjoy, and thank you!

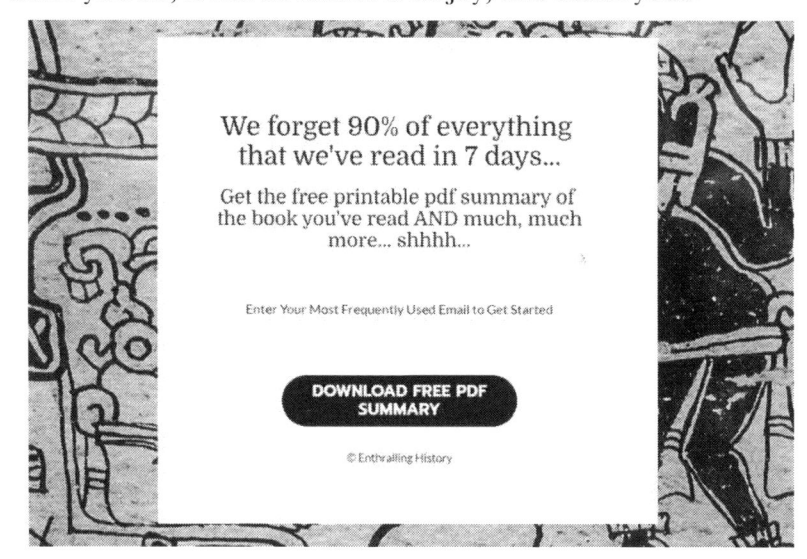

Bibliography

Addis, F. (2020). *The Eternal City: A History of Rome* (Reprint ed.). Pegasus Books.

Ambler, J. L. (n.d.). Introduction to ancient Roman art (article). Khan Academy. *https://www.khanacademy.org/humanities/ancient-art-civilizations/roman/beginners-guide-rome/a/introduction-to-ancient-roman-art*

Andrews, E. (2022, July 21). 8 Ways Roads Helped Rome Rule the Ancient World. HISTORY. *https://www.history.com/news/8-ways-roads-helped-rome-rule-the-ancient-world*

Augustus Closes the Temple of Janus. (2019, October 10). History Today. *https://www.historytoday.com/archive/foundations/augustus-closes-temple-janus*

Bileta, V. (2021, July 9). Rome Halts the Huns: The Battle of Châlons (Catalaunian Plains). TheCollector. *https://www.thecollector.com/the-decisive-battle-of-chalons-catalaunian-plains-an-in-depth-review/*

Campbell, C. J. (2022, March 24). Peace & Prosperity: What Was the Pax Romana? TheCollector. *https://www.thecollector.com/what-was-pax-romana/*

Cartwright, M. (2022, July 30). Roman Roads. World History Encyclopedia. *https://www.worldhistory.org/article/758/roman-roads/*

Cartwright, M. (2022, July 31). Roman Baths. World History Encyclopedia. *https://www.worldhistory.org/Roman_Baths/*

Cartwright, M. (2022, July 31). Roman Siege Warfare. World History Encyclopedia. *https://www.worldhistory.org/Roman_Siege_Warfare/*

Cartwright, M. (2022, August 1). Circus Maximus. World History Encyclopedia. *https://www.worldhistory.org/Circus_Maximus/*

Cartwright, M. (2022, August 1). Praetorian Guard. World History Encyclopedia. *https://www.worldhistory.org/Praetorian_Guard/*

Cartwright, M. (2022, August 1). Roman Senate. World History Encyclopedia. *https://www.worldhistory.org/Roman_Senate/*

The Cursus publicus: The Courier Service of the Roman Empire: History of Information. (n.d.). History of Information. *https://www.historyofinformation.com/detail.php?id=1394*

Gill, N. S. (2018, March 17). What Was Life Like During the Pax Romana? ThoughtCo. *https://www.thoughtco.com/what-was-the-pax-romana-120829*

Jasiński, J. (2022, June 29). Scutum. IMPERIUM ROMANUM. *https://imperiumromanum.pl/en/roman-army/equipment-of-roman-legionary/scutum/*

Klein, C. (2022, July 21). How Ancient Rome Thrived During Pax Romana. HISTORY. *https://www.history.com/news/pax-romana-roman-empire-peace-augustus*

Land, G. (2018, August 9). Trade and Transport at the Height of the Roman Empire. History Hit. *https://www.historyhit.com/trade-and-transport-at-the-height-of-the-roman-empire/*

Mark, J. J. (2021, July 31). Ancient Roman Society. World History Encyclopedia. *https://www.worldhistory.org/article/1463/ancient-roman-society/*

Mark, J. J. (2022, August 1). Vestal Virgin. World History Encyclopedia. *https://www.worldhistory.org/Vestal_Virgin/*

PBS. (n.d.). The Roman Empire: in the First Century. The Roman Empire. Social Order. Slaves & Freemen | PBS. *https://www.pbs.org/empires/romans/empire/slaves_freemen.html*

Preskar, P. (2021, December 30). The Praetorian Guard —Power, Greed, and Terror | History of Yesterday. Medium.

Provincial Government of the Roman Empire | UNRV.com Roman History. (n.d.). UNRV History. *https://www.unrv.com/government/provincialgovernment.php*

Ricketts, C. (2018, July 25). 5 Important Roman Siege Engines. History Hit. *https://www.historyhit.com/important-roman-siege-engines/*

Ricketts, C. (2018, July 30). Divorce and Decline: The Division of East and West Roman Empires. History Hit. https://www.historyhit.com/divorce-and-decline-the-division-of-east-and-west-roman-empires/

Ricketts, C. (2018, August 9). The Growth of Christianity in the Roman Empire. History Hit. https://www.historyhit.com/the-growth-of-christianity-in-the-roman-empire/

Roman Carriages. (n.d.). Vita Romae. https://www.vita-romae.com/roman-carriages.html

The Roman Empire and Trade. (2015). History Learning. https://historylearning.com/a-history-of-ancient-rome/the-roman-empire-and-trade/

Roman Roads. (n.d.). Vita Romae. https://www.vita-romae.com/roman-roads.html

Severus: Rome's first African Emperor. (n.d.). Sky HISTORY TV Channel. https://www.history.co.uk/article/severus-rome%E2%80%99s-first-african-emperor

Warfare History Network. (2022, July 14). The Roman Gladius. https://warfarehistorynetwork.com/article/the-roman-gladius/

Wasson, D. L. (2022, July 30). Roman Emperor. World History Encyclopedia. https://www.worldhistory.org/Roman_Emperor/

Wasson, D. L. (2022, July 31). Constantine I. World History Encyclopedia. https://www.worldhistory.org/Constantine_I/

Wikipedia contributors. (2022, April 11). Temple of Janus (Roman Forum). Wikipedia. https://en.wikipedia.org/wiki/Temple_of_Janus_(Roman_Forum)

Wikipedia contributors. (2022, May 27). Peregrinus (Roman). Wikipedia. https://en.wikipedia.org/wiki/Peregrinus_(Roman)

Wikipedia contributors. (2022, June 25). Pax Romana. Wikipedia. https://en.wikipedia.org/wiki/Pax_Romana

Wikipedia contributors. (2022, July 19). Testudo formation. Wikipedia. https://en.wikipedia.org/wiki/Testudo_formation

Wikipedia contributors. (2022, July 27). Baths of Caracalla. Wikipedia. https://en.wikipedia.org/wiki/Baths_of_Caracalla

Wikipedia contributors. (2022, July 29). Roman Forum. Wikipedia. https://en.wikipedia.org/wiki/Roman_Forum

Wikipedia contributors. (2022, July 30). Marian reforms. Wikipedia. https://en.wikipedia.org/wiki/Marian_reforms#Marian_reforms

Williams, J. A. (2022, May 6). What life as a Roman emperor was really like. Grunge.Com. *https://www.grunge.com/855148/what-life-as-a-roman-emperor-was-really-like/*

Printed in Great Britain
by Amazon

8a83bdcd-9c58-419d-9b46-b195a58cb511R01